DOKTOR SNAKE'S
VOODOO
SPELLBOOK

DOKTOR SNAKE'S

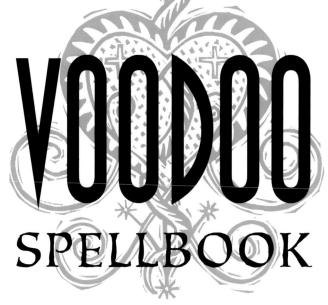

VOODOO

SPELLBOOK

Spells, curses and folk magic
for all your needs

St. Martin's Griffin
New York

This book is dedicated to the memory of Earl Marlowe, a magical man and keeper of the lore.

Text copyright © Doktor Snake 2000
Illustrations copyright © Chris Daunt 2000
This edition copyright © Eddison Sadd Editions 2000

Manufactured in Hong Kong. All rights reserved. No part of this book may be used or reproduced in any manner whatsoever without written permission except in the case of brief quotations embodied in critical articles or reviews. For information, address St. Martin's Press, 175 Fifth Avenue, New York, NY 10010.

The right of Doktor Snake to be identified as the author of the work has been asserted by him in accordance with the Copyright, Designs and Patents Act 1988.

A catalogue record for this book is available from the Library of Congress.

ISBN 0-312-26509-3

First Edition: 2000

3   5   7   9   10   8   6   4   2

AN EDDISON • SADD EDITION
Edited, designed and produced by
Eddison Sadd Editions Limited
St Chad's House, 148 King's Cross Road
London WC1X 9DH

Phototypeset in Anna and Bernhard Modern BT using QuarkXPress on Apple Macintosh
Origination by Bright Arts PTE, Singapore
Printed by Sing Cheong Printing Co. Ltd, Hong Kong

CONTENTS

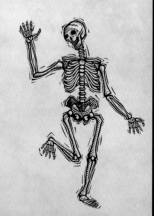

Introduction

SONG OF THE SNAKE

*'Hoodoo is about having a
healthy disregard for the impossible.'*

Dr Snake to the Alliance of Magicians, Mystics and Outlaws, Miami, 1997

Greetings! I'm Doktor Snake, a conjure man living on the east side of paradise, where a Hoodoo sun shines and a lucky mojo rain falls. I'm sitting here on my back porch, guitar in hand, tape deck set to record, reciting stories, spells and conjure formulas from the Hoodoo and Voodoo tradition, putting them all together to make up a book – the book you're now holding in your hands.

My spellbook draws much of its inspiration from the various strands of Afro-American and Afro-Caribbean spirituality – Voodoo, Santeria and Macumba, in particular. Primarily, however, it is a book of folk magic, or 'Hoodoo' as it is called in the American South. Hoodoo magic unashamedly places great emphasis on the attainment of personal magic power. Practitioners of Hoodoo never sit back and accept their lot in life; they change it as they see fit using sorcery or 'conjure'. Accordingly, the core attitude of my spellbook is practicality. It gets you started in casting spells that will help you gain money and prosperity, love and sex, and health and well-being. You will also be empowered to bring back a lost lover, repel enemies and avert the evil eye. However, before you can achieve these ends, you will need to learn the basics of the art of conjure. Therefore I give clear instruction on how to use roots, potions and herbal baths; how to construct Voodoo dolls and lucky mojo talismans; and how to set up a simple altar. With

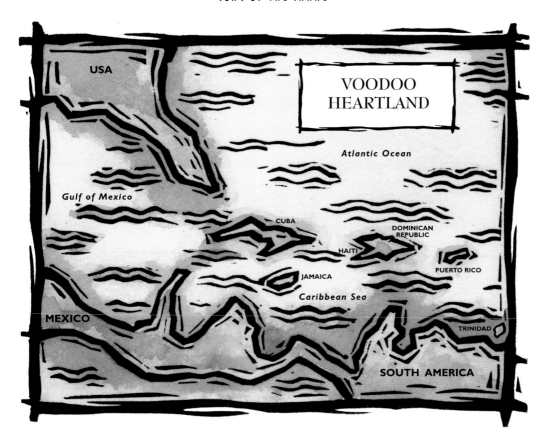

these spells, potions and magical recipes, you will have the knowledge to gain personal power beyond your wildest imaginings.

Besides giving instruction in the art of conjure, my spellbook relates numerous anecdotes and stories concerning actual practitioners of Hoodoo and Voodoo sorcery. It also takes a brief look at the many myths and legends which underpin New World magic and religion. I humbly hope that this book will act as a catalyst, leading you to discover a rich and diverse spirit way which is open to all, no matter what your colour or creed.

ORIGINS

The system of folk magic outlined in this book has its roots in African magic and religion, which arrived in the New World between the sixteenth and nineteenth centuries with the slaves. In a bid to avoid persecution for their pagan beliefs, the slaves superimposed their gods onto the Christianity of their masters. This fusion led to the formation of various spiritual traditions. In Brazil it gave birth to Macumba and Candomble; in Cuba to Santeria and Nyannego; in Jamaica to Bongoism and African Cumina (also known as Maroon Dance); in Trinidad to Shango; in Haiti to Voudoun (Voodoo); and in the United States to Hoodoo. Many other influences played an integral part in the formation of these religions. South American Indian beliefs, for instance, along with the Spiritism of Allan Kardec, popular in the late nineteenth century, had key roles in the development of Macumba in Brazil; while the Jewish and pagan folklore of the European immigrants to the United States, coupled with the plant and herb lore of Native American shamanism, featured strongly in Hoodoo folk magic practice.

SECRET POWER

An important element in New World sorcery is the belief that names are imbued with magical power. In *The African Presence in Caribbean Literature*, Edward Kamau Braithwaite explains, 'People feel a name is so important that a change in his name could transform a person's life.' Faith in the secret power of the name is nowhere more evident than in Hoodoo magic. It is the reason why Hoodoo doctors adopt animal names such as Dr Crow and Dr Snake (like the African witch doctor, they assume the name of the bird or beast from which they draw their power). For the Hoodoo doctor, taking on a new name is a way of shaping personal destiny. Similarly, blues musicians like Muddy Waters, Lightnin' Hopkins and Howlin' Wolf took on their names as an act of magical transformation.

MAGICAL MANTLE

As we've seen, New World magic has its roots in Africa. Yet white people have also been practitioners of this ancient art. One of the most famous was Ed McTeer whom you will meet in Chapter Five.

I myself am a white man. I came to the conjure path due to playing guitar in a band with a Trinidadian singer and Hoodooist called Earl Marlowe. When I first knew him, Earl looked to be in his early sixties (although he claimed to be 127). He was a very picturesque character. His head was shaved and he regularly wore purple-tinted aviator sunglasses. Sometimes he would wear sharp Italian suits, other times colourful African robes.

During our association together, Earl told me many sorcery-related stories about the Caribbean and the American South (where he lived before settling in England). He also taught me much about the trade of the Hoodoo doctor. This, coupled with my own study of African and New World religion, proved invaluable as, after Earl died, many of his clients came to me asking for help.

At first I was reluctant, lacking confidence in my abilities. But then a friend of Earl, an old West Indian guy who ran a domino club, said to me, 'Earl handed his mantle down to you. You might not know it, but he did.' With that, he gave me a silver snake ring, telling me that Earl had entrusted it to him just before he left this world, with instructions that it be given to me. After that, I spent two weeks in deep meditation, burning oils and incenses, and communing with the spirits. The result was that I took the magical name Dr Snake and became a professional witch doctor.

Doktor Snake
The Name with No Man

Chapter One

THE ART OF CONJURE

*'Anything may be conjure
and nothing may be conjure ...'*

Zora Neale Hurston, *Mules and Men*, 1935

To become adept at Voodoo sorcery requires you learn a degree of mind control. You must tame those wayward thoughts and impulses that lead you into all sorts of trouble or unwanted situations. In short, you must learn to be impeccable and unshakable in your words and actions on this earth. At the same time, however, you must maintain the ability to be spontaneous; to speak and act as the spirit dictates. All this requires a precarious mental balance. But this 'poise of the mind' can certainly be attained through the practice of Hoodoo conjuration.

VOODOO TRANCE

To get started in the art of conjure you first need to learn how to enter a state of trance. Trance puts you in touch with your unconscious mind, which is the wellspring of instinctive and intuitive wisdom. The unconscious mind believes wholeheartedly in magic and the supernatural; whereas its rational and material-istic counterpart, the conscious mind – or 'ego-self' – does not.

To execute magic successfully, we need to believe in it 100 per cent. Therefore we must escape the rationalistic confines of the conscious mind and, through trance, enter the visionary world of the unconscious mind. My Hoodoo mentor, Earl Marlowe, put it this way, 'You gotta believe for the magic to work. Don't matter if no one else believes, so long as you do. If you don't believe, and you wanna work conjure, you gotta keep mesmerizin' yourself till you do believe.'

Trance can also be used to gain contact with the spirits. In fact, what marks out a fully-fledged conjuror is his or her ability to see, hear and deal construc-tively with the spirits. When you contact with the spirits is when you really start getting things done.

The main method I use for entering a state of trance was taught to me by Earl. It is straightforward and can easily be mastered by the beginner. In fact, once you have done it a few times, you no longer need to go through the ritual of it. You just have to think, 'I'll go into trance now', and you're in. As long as circumstances allow, always go into trance before commencing ritual or spell work.

When you perform sorcery, it is important to ensure the chatter of your mind is stilled. You don't want your inner-voice distracting you with the concerns of the day. By focusing attention, trance induction techniques facilitate the stilling of the internal dialogue. So if you get distracted by your inner-voice when performing spell work, simply re-run whatever trance induction you used.

HOW TO ENTER TRANCE

1. Sit down comfortably and relax. A good way to achieve a state of relaxation quickly is to make your out-breaths a little longer than your in-breaths.

2. Find something to fix your gaze on. Try using a candle flame or a crystal – any convenient object will do.

3. Now make three statements (out loud or to yourself) about what you can see. This is your visual experience. If your gaze is fixed on a candle, you might say, 'I see a coloured halo around the flame.'

4. Make three statements about what you can hear. This is your auditory experience. You might say, 'I hear the birds singing outside my window' or 'I hear the sound of my breath as I inhale and exhale.'

Trance relaxes your body and mind and can be used to contact the spirits during ritual or spell work.

5. Make three statements about what you can feel. This is your kinaesthetic experience. You might say, 'I feel the warmth of my hands resting on my thighs.'

6. Run through each of the three primary senses again, making two, then one, new statement about each. If your eyes get drowsy, allow them to close and substitute internal visualization (what you see in your mind's eye) for external.

7. Now perform your ritual – gently opening your eyes if they closed during the induction. When your ritual is complete, you can come out of the hypnotic state by simply counting down from five to one and saying 'Wake up!'

Using this technique, most people drift into a trance very quickly, usually before they have finished the second or third run through the sensory channels. You will know you are in a trance when a mild 'dreaminess' overtakes you and visions begin to flow past your mind's eye. Don't worry about the apparent 'depth' of your trance; sometimes it will seem deep and profound, other times mild. The main thing is that you feel relaxed and at ease.

SKELETON DANCE

Earl taught me another good method for inducing a state of trance. He called it the 'Skeleton Dance' because it involves 'dancing' the focus of your attention over your bones.

'What you do is simple,' he said. 'You imagine your skeleton and then, starting with the toes, picture in your mind's eye each bone in your body. From the toes you work your way up both legs at once. Flow into the pelvis. Shoot up the spine. Swoop across the ribs. Sail down the arms; ride back up to the shoulders, then up the neck to the skull, and right into the centre of the brain – which, from a medical textbook point of view, isn't a bone, but wha'da they know?'

The Skeleton Dance is a technique that has long been used, in one form or another, by spiritual traditions worldwide; in fact, it can be traced back to shamans in Palaeolithic times. The fact that Earl used it simply shows that Hoodoo and Voodoo workers use whatever works in their magic.

HOODOO ALTAR

Once you are proficient at entering trance and at stopping the internal dialogue, it is time to set up a Hoodoo altar. The altar serves as your own personal microcosm of the vast macrocosm of the multiverse. It is your small doorway into the magnitude of creation. If the spirits are willing, it may be possible for your spiritual self to step right through this doorway and enter the astral world. Once there, you may learn something of the incomprehensible secrets of how Nature and the cosmos work. If this is the case, this knowledge will enable you to use

your altar as a focus for manipulating aspects of fate and destiny, both in your own life and in the lives of people you do spells or jobs for.

Even if the spirits do not decree that you learn the secrets of the astral world, you can still utilize a Hoodoo altar for performing conjure and spells that will enhance your life and the lives of those around you.

SETTING UP YOUR ALTAR

Any flat surface can be used for an altar – a wooden box, tea chest, coffee table, a piece of board propped up on bricks. Most convenient, however, is a dressing table, partly because it is the ideal size, and also because your ritual supplies can be stored in the top drawer.

Here is a list of items for a basic Hoodoo altar set-up. This list is a guide, not the written law. Please feel free to use your intuition, combined with solid research, to come up with your own individual methods of working. There is only one rule in Voodoo and Hoodoo: use whatever works for you.

White Candle This signifies the positive forces inherent within the multiverse.

Black Candle This signifies the negative forces inherent within the multiverse.

Glass Tumbler Fill this with spring water and Witch's Salt (*available from suppliers, see page 125*) and place it between the white and black candles. It signifies the 'grey' area, or equilibrium point, between the positive and negative forces of creation that are represented by the black and white candles. The Witch's Salt, for me at least, symbolizes the magic worker, or 'seer', who can perceive these

OPPOSITE *Set up your Hoodoo altar with all your magical equipment. If you like, cover the altar with a cloth – choose whatever colour or design inspires you.*

invisible polarities as they flow throughout the multiverse, continually combining and separating as they do so.

Tin foil Place a strip of this under figurine candles, so the dripping wax doesn't damage the surface you are working on.

Knife Use a sharp knife to trim candles, wood and roots.

Saucers or plates Two or three saucers or plates will come in handy as makeshift candleholders.

Candle snuffer Always use a candle snuffer to put out candles – *never* blow them out.

Incense burner You can buy incense burners from spiritual supply stores or New Age shops. However, any heat-resistant dish or bowl, the size of a cup, will do fine (if not better). This should be half-filled with sand or earth. The sand or earth will absorb the heat generated from the burning incense and will prevent scorching your altar. Then break up a tablet of charcoal (available from spiritual supply stores), into the burner. Use a taper to light the charcoal and sprinkle the incense or herbs of your choice on top of the smouldering embers. As a convenient alternative, you can use self-lighting incense.

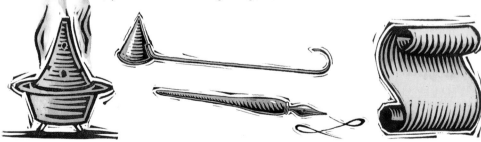

Dip pen and inks These are used for writing out your magical intentions and requests during spell workings. Appropriate inks to use are Dragon's Blood Ink or Dove's Blood Ink. Some conjure workers use their own blood.

Parchment paper You write your requests on parchment paper and then place them under a candle during rituals. I use top-quality writing paper, but sheepskin parchment is more traditional.

Holy water Use this to bless and purify your magical tools and the area you are working in. Holy water can be purchased from religious or spiritual supply stores. Alternatively, you can make it yourself *(see page 18)*.

Nails Use 4 or 5 inch nails (about 12 cm) to write on candles. Make sure you have plenty of brand-new nails as you need to use a different nail for each spell.

Scales These are handy for weighing out quantities of herbs, roots and powders.

Pestle and mortar These are ideal for grinding up herbs before using them.

Other supplies You will need a supply of candles, incenses, oils, powders and herbs. You will hear these mentioned throughout the spellbook, and they are all available from suppliers *(see page 125)*.

⚊ HOLY WATER ⚊

Holy water is used to purify, or consecrate, your Voodoo altar. It can be bought from any spiritual or church supply store, but to make your own is just as effective. All you need is some sea salt and a bowl of spring water.

First put a tablespoon of sea salt in a saucer (1). Then hold both hands, palms down, over the salt. Visualize white light flowing from the bright blue skies above, through your head and body, and out through your palms into the salt. As you do so, recite the chant (1). Now hold both hands, palms down, over your bowl of spring water (2). Again visualize a white light flowing through you and out through your palms into the water. This time repeat chant (2). Next, slowly pour the salt into the spring water (3) and stir the mixture, while intoning chant (3).

(1)

*'Blessed be,
this salt of the sea,
may everything it touches
be pure and true.'*

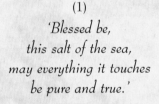

(2)

*'Primed and ready,
this water of life,
may all it touches
be cleansed right through.'*

(3)

*'Salt and water,
holy and blessed,
cast out evil from
all you touch.'*

PURIFICATION

Before proceeding further, you must purify or bless your magical tools. This both removes all unwanted influences from them and charges them with numinous power. You can either pass the items through incense smoke or sprinkle them with holy water *(see opposite)*. You only need to purify your magical tools once, but do ensure that all new items are purified before you use them.

If you pass your magical equipment through incense smoke, then burn Blessing Incense or Purification Incense, or alternatively burn dried thyme (a good cleansing herb), and repeat chant (1). If you decide to sprinkle your magical tools with holy water, then repeat chant (2). If you are of the Catholic faith (as many Voodooists are), then feel free to substitute 'O Spirits' for something more appropriate, such as 'O Almighty God', 'O Lord Jesus' or 'Our Lady'.

Once the altar tools have been purified, you can set them out in an aesthetically pleasing manner on the altar. As a guideline, I suggest putting the black candle on the right-hand side at the back and the white candle on the left-hand side. Place the tumbler of spring water and Witch's Salt centrally between the two. Everything else should be neatly arranged around the altar. Remember to leave room for the various ingredients that will later be required for specific spells or jobs. A nice addition to any altar layout is a vase of fresh flowers.

(1)
'O Spirits, as I offer up this incense for your blessings, please cleanse these tools and remove all unwanted influences from them. O Spirits, please also imbue these items with magical power.'

(2)
'O Spirits, as I sprinkle this holy water, please banish all negativity from these magical tools and instil them with spiritual power.'

OPENING RITUAL

In works of magic – having first entered trance – you need to perform an opening ritual. This cleanses the area you are working in and blocks out all unwanted forces, such as malevolent spirits or simply the worries of the day. It also puts you in a meditative frame of mind, conducive to performing sorcery.

First, take the bottle of holy water and sprinkle some over all four corners of the room and around your altar area. As you do so, say something along the lines of chant (1) at the foot of the page.

Then light your candles (white first, then black) and then your incense. You are now ready to cast your spell. If you are not doing a spell, you could meditate or pray at this point. In which case, burn Meditation Incense or Holy Incense.

CLOSING RITUAL

When your conjure working or meditation session is completed, you will need to perform a closing ritual. This simply entails pausing for a moment and giving thanks. You could hold out your hands over the altar, palms facing down, and say a chant like chant (2), below.

Extinguish the candles in the reverse order of lighting them. Then do a final sprinkling of the altar and the surrounding room with holy water.

(1)

'With this holy water,
I banish all forces,
that are not in harmony with me.'

(2)

'I thank all the spirits and other forces
which have helped me in this ritual.
Let us go our separate ways in love
and peace.'

⌐ HYSSOP CLEANSING BATH ⌐

Before and after doing spell workings, many Hoodooists and Voodooists take a ritual cleansing bath. If you do decide to do this, then I suggest taking a herbal bath made with hyssop; it cleanses and removes negativity from the body. Place 3–4 teaspoons of dried hyssop in a cup. Pour boiling water over the herb, then cover and leave for 20 minutes. When the mixture is ready, pour it into your bath, chanting:

'Holy Hyssop,
cleanse me to the core,
and drive all evil
from my door.'

You can also use fresh hyssop. It is frequently cultivated and can be found growing wild in warm countries. On a medicinal level, hyssop is a cleansing herb. It relieves catarrh and reduces secretion of mucus, as well as regulating blood pressure (high or low) and calming the nerves. Please note that hyssop should not be used in pregnancy or if you suffer from epilepsy.

A convenient alternative to the dried or fresh herb is the ready-prepared Dr Pryor's Hyssop Bath Oil *(see suppliers, page 125).*

Hyssop is an aromatic plant with long, tapering
leaves and clusters of flowers.

⁃ CANDLE MAGIC ⁃

Many spells use candles, and it is important to ensure that they are burnt safely, especially when they must be left to burn down after the ritual. The colour of the candle used is dictated by the intent of your spell. There are no hard and fast rules, but the following correspond to the ideas of most practitioners.

Red *Love, sex, passion, affection, physical vitality.*

Green *Money, gambling luck, business, regular work, good crops.*

White *Spiritual blessings, purity, healing, rest.*

Black *Repelling, dark thoughts, sorrow, freedom from evil.*

Purple *Mastery, power, ambition, control, command.*

Pink *Attraction, romance, clean living.*

Orange *Change of plans, opening the way, prophetic dreams.*

Yellow *Devotion, prayer, money (gold), cheerfulness, attraction.*

Light blue *Peace, harmony, joy, kind intentions.*

Dark blue *Moodiness, depression, unfortunate circumstances.*

Brown *Court cases, neutrality.*

Red and black (red inside, black outside) *Return evil to the sender.*

ANOINTING CANDLES

When you have chosen a candle for your spell *(see opposite)*, you need to anoint it with an appropriate oil (for example, Love Oil for a love spell or Damnation Oil for a curse). Rub the oil from the base to the wick, working away from yourself, in works of repelling or cursing; and rub towards yourself, from the wick to the base, in works of attraction. To add to the power of a candle after it has been anointed, sprinkle it with an appropriate powder (such as Love Powder for a love candle). During the anointing process, visualize the intent of the job or spell in your mind's eye. It is also very important to use only one candle for one purpose and to burn it to the bottom. Never use the same candle for different jobs.

WHEN TO DO RITUALS

An integral part of conjure work is deciding on the most appropriate time to perform spells. The phases of the moon are an important factor to consider. The waxing moon is best for works of increase and of a constructive nature, such as gaining money, love and good health. The waning moon is best for works of lessening or of destruction, such as decreasing poverty, getting rid of unwanted people or cursing. The full moon is usually seen as a time of great power and, accordingly, many practitioners do major rituals at that time.

The Reverend Gary Fox, a Voodoo worker living in Texas, insists that black magic is best done during the dark of the moon. 'Some say you should do black work at full moon, but that's a crock o' pig shit. Dark o' the moon's when you wanna do it. A year or so back, I had trouble with some neighbours of mine – they kept swarmin' onto my land like pesky varmints. I tried everything to make 'em move out – even tried dynamitin' 'em out. Nothin' worked. So I did a little black work one midnight at the dark of the moon and they were out like mules with scud missiles up their asses.'

As well as taking into account the phases of the moon, some Hoodooists, including myself, decide the timing for ritual work according to the position of the hands on the clock. Works of constructive magic and increase are best done when both hands on the clock are rising. And works of destruction and decrease are best performed when both hands on the clock are falling. So, for example, if you want to gain wealth, then do your ritual when the moon is waxing at a time when both hands on your clock are rising – say, between 8.30 and 9.00 in the morning (this time of day has the added advantage that the day itself is also waxing). Alternatively, midnight – the 'witching hour' – is a good time for all works of powerful magic, whether constructive or destructive.

For major workings, the time of the year can also be taken into account. Spring is the waxing of the year and so would be the ideal time to begin a ritual intended to win you a lottery jackpot. The culmination of the ritual could be timed for midsummer's day, just before the year begins to wane.

During autumn, the waning of the year, you could perform a spell to rid yourself of negative patterns of thinking, and have midwinter's day, the very dead of winter, as the final banishing of these patterns. Then, somewhere around the first of February, you could ritually 'plant' the seeds of positive thinking and by harvest time of that year, your life will be transformed.

Once you have decided on the timing of a ritual, perform it, if possible, at the same time on each consecutive day until the ritual is complete.

SINGING TURTLE

Once you have taken up the path of Hoodoo, it is advisable to maintain a certain air of privacy. Try not to be a blabbermouth. There is no harm in talking a lot, especially if you are naturally gregarious, but it is good to keep a check on your tongue when it comes to deeper things. Not everyone respects the ways of the Hoodoos, so the less they know about your beliefs and practices, the better. Earl Marlowe once told me a tale relevant to this point. He'd heard it many years ago in Louisiana, but the story's roots, he assured me, lay in Africa. As we sat on a bench overlooking a section of the River Lea in East London, Earl toked heavily on a joint, and in his deep Caribbean-tinged drawl proceeded to tell me the tale of the singing turtle.

'One day, while out fishin', a boy saw a turtle crawlin' on a log in the river. It had a banjo, and 'fore long it sat up and began pickin' a tune on the instrument and singin' a soulful melody. The boy ran home and told his father, who gave

him a thrashin' for tellin' a lie. Finally, the boy persuaded his father to go and see the turtle playin' the banjo and singin'. When they got there, the turtle wasn't to be seen, and the father was ready to thrash the boy again. But then, all of a sudden, they heard music and saw the turtle on the log, pickin' out a riff on its banjo and singin' these lyrics, "Live in peace. Don't tell all you see."'

Chapter Two

MAGIC MONEY

*'I've been using the (money) oil about ten years,
and I've been winning.'*

Joseph Bush, successful pool shooter, quoted during the 1970s

As we sat in a tiny Italian café in the King's Cross area of London, Earl turned to me, 'If you wanna get seriously rich, what you need is magic money.'

'Magic money?!' I exclaimed, with a grin.

'Ain't no joke,' replied Earl, with a dismissive sweep of his hand. 'Might be as elusive as a four-leafed clover, but magic money is out there in circulation. If you get some in your change, or find some in your pocket, you'll be made for life.'

'What does it look like?'

'Same as ordinary money. Feels different, though.'

'In what way?'

'Feels hot. But you have to have the power to tell the difference. It's spirit money, y'see.'

Although the very idea of all this seemed absurd, my interest had been piqued. I lit a Cuban cigar, then asked, 'When you say it's spirit money, do you mean spirits give it to you?'

'I mean just that,' he replied. 'When you're least expecting it, a spirit will pop up out of nowhere and give you magic money. It might take the guise of a store-assistant and give you a spirit coin in your change. Believe me, that assistant wouldn't be human; he or she would be a spirit. If you went back to the store the next day to find the spirit again, they wouldn't be there. You could describe them to the other staff working there, but they'd say you must have been mistaken, because no one of that description works in the store. Most people don't recognize a spirit when they see one because it will look human, like anyone in the street. But if you got the sight, you know it's a spirit.'

Earl pulled out a hip flask and poured some dark rum into his black coffee. He then went on to tell me that all big lottery or gambling winners have magic money somewhere on their person before winning. They wouldn't be consciously aware that they had magic money in their possession, he explained, but some sixth sense would tell them not to spend it or pass it on. However, these are exceptional individuals; when the average person gets magic money, they simply spend it, which means someone else gets rich instead of them.

'Is there any way you can force the issue – I mean, can you obtain magic money using sorcery?' I asked, in the hope of finding a fast route to a lottery win myself.

He shook his head. 'Very rarely. Some have done it. But usually it either happens or it doesn't – and if it does happen, then it will only happen once in your life, and in very, very exceptional cases, twice.'

'But can you use sorcery to get a bit of money generally?' I asked.

'Yeah, you can use it to meet your needs,' he replied.

Earl had never had a big lottery win. But through conjure work, he maintained a good lifestyle on a low income. His needs were small and he seemed to draw money from the proverbial 'ether' whenever he needed it.

CASH COLLECTOR

Earl had a favourite money spell, which he called the 'Cash Collector'. It can be used to good effect in all circumstances where money is required. You will need the following ingredients.

1 teaspoon of frankincense
⅔ teaspoon of clove powder
⅔ teaspoon of bayberry root chips
⅔ teaspoon of archangel herb (angelica)
½ teaspoon of cinnamon powder
A pinch of saltpetre
A pinch of Money Powder

Once you have obtained your ingredients, set up your altar. Burn some Money Drawing Incense and light a green candle (1). Blend all the ingredients

(1) (2) (3)

thoroughly and place them in a green flannel mojo bag (2). A mojo bag is tradi-tionally a small charm bag, with a white drawstring, that can either be made at home or obtained from a spiritual supply store. Sew the top tightly shut and then sprinkle the bag with 9 drops of Money Oil (a green, perfumed oil). Attach a string or cord to the charm and wear it around your neck (3), or carry it in a purse or pocket at all times.

To further aid you in finding money, blend the same amount of the above mixture and place it on a plain white saucer. Burn half of it each morning on rising, and the other half each night before going to bed. This creates favourable money vibrations throughout your place of residence.

Bayberry root chips can also be sprinkled on the money in your wallet to attract more money and good fortune to you.

CHARLES THE GRINDER

When I first met him in 1981, Earl claimed to be 127 years old. I just accepted this and enjoyed the many stories he told me about the people he knew around the turn of the century. One particular story concerned a New Orleans Voodoo doctor called Charles the Grinder, who supposedly taught Earl money magic way back in 1905.

At that time, Charles the Grinder was a well-known face around West Baton Rouge parish. He would travel around the plantations and villages in the area offering to sharpen scissors, knives, tools and ploughs – anything that needed sharpening. But he wasn't the industrious man he might at first appear to be. Charles never worked for more than half a day at a time, his maxim being, 'A man who works half-time, lives twice-time, and in relaxation there is double expectation, scientifically speaking.' Loosely translated, this meant that the man who takes it easy in life, lives twice as long as the hardworking and ambitious man.

Of course, with this kind of attitude it helps if you are adept at money conjure – and Charles the Grinder undoubtedly was. His sharpening business, which was lucrative in itself, was in fact a cover for a thriving conjure business. Through this, he made at least ten times as much money as any labourer in those days could hope to. Charles first got started in conjure when, as a seaman, he spent some years in Haiti, where he learned all about Voodoo magic. 'When I got back,' he told Earl, 'I taught all the big Voodoos in New Orleans everything they know 'bout Voodoo. In the end, though, they ran me outa the city 'cause of my superior knowledge.'

Earl spent six months with Charles the Grinder living on his houseboat on the Mississippi River. Charles kept an enormous stock of conjure paraphernalia on board, including all sorts of shells, fish bones and the skulls of small animals. Some of these were gilded; others stained black or purple. All of these items were sold around the plantations and villages as good-luck charms, which are known as 'gris-gris' around New Orleans. The most expensive gris-gris he stocked were made from the dried bladders of hogs, which he'd gather from the plantations at hog-killing times. These he sold for $2.50 each, and they were used almost exclusively for wreaking terrible curses on people.

Charles also kept a pet on the boat – a rooster with golden feathers. 'It was tame as a cat, but fat as a pig,' recalled Earl. 'When it flapped its wings, it spread gold dust on the floor. Charles always said the dust was pure gold, and that the rooster was a golden legend. What he meant by that, no one ever knew.'

One time, Earl was looking at the gold-dust-producing rooster and got to thinking that he'd had enough of being poor, and that it was high time he had a share of the wealth in the world. Only problem was, Earl didn't relish the prospect of hard work.

As might be expected, when he raised this point with Charles, he was very sympathetic and, without hesitation, said he would personally help Earl work some serious money conjure.

➤ HIGH JOHN THE CONQUEROR ROOT ➤

A central ingredient in many African-American money spells is High John the Conqueror root. John the Conqueror was reputedly a black slave who, by wit and humour, always got one over on his slave masters. In folkloric terms, he was very much related to the trickster figure, Brer Rabbit, and to similar characters whose origins lay in African myth and legend. John the Conqueror root is named after him for it carries his luck.

The plant from which the root comes is 'Tormentil' *(Potentilla erecta)*. It is a downy perennial plant, with serrated leaves and four-petalled yellow flowers, which is used in medicine, tanning and dyeing. To obtain the maximum magical results from the root, it is customary to 'fix' it, so it can be carried in the pocket as a money charm or put in a mojo hand (charm bag) with other ingredients. Here are two ways a root can be fixed.

FOR DRAWING MONEY TO YOU

Anoint your root with John the Conqueror Oil, taking care to thoroughly rub the oil in. Then wrap your paper money around the root and keep it in your pocket. This type of charm is often referred to as a 'pocket piece'.

FOR LUCK IN GAMBLING

Fill a mojo bag (red flannel for success or green flannel for money) with a Lucky Hand root, a pinch of Five Finger grass, a pair of (red or green) dice and a High John the Conqueror root. You can then add either a dried bat's heart, a rabbit's foot or an alligator's tooth. Anoint the mojo bag with red Fast Luck Oil, John the Conqueror Oil or your lover's urine, and always carry it on your person when you go out gambling.

JEZEBEL SPELL

A couple of days later, Charles said that it was time to do the job. 'Moon's waxin' and the spirits is willin'.' With that, he went to one of his many cupboards and pulled out a large green candle, a small bottle of oil and a gnarled-looking root he called the 'Jezebel Root'. He then instructed Earl to anoint the candle with oil. 'It's Money Drawin' Oil – made outa holy frankincense, myrrh and sandalwood, with a little bayberry herb thrown in,' he said. 'You'd do well to remember that, man, cause ain't many root doctors willin' to share their secrets.'

When Earl had anointed the candle (rubbing towards himself, from wick to base), Charles got him to place the candle in a plain white saucer and light it. Charles then produced a bottle of moonshine whiskey. 'We gotta wait till it burns down,' he said, 'so we may as well take a sip or two of sour mash to pass the time.'

When at last the candle had burned down, Charles instructed Earl to push the Jezebel root into the middle of the soft candle wax and to roll up the wax into a ball. He then had to leave it in a cool place to harden. While they waited for this to occur, the two got back to drinking.

Half-an-hour later, Charles leaped from his chair, 'Wax'll be hard now. Come on, we gotta head straight for the cemetery and drop it into a fresh-dug grave.'

When the now somewhat intoxicated pair arrived at the local cemetery, Earl, on Charles' instructions, dropped the wax ball into a freshly dug grave and intoned the incantation below three times.

'Jezebel, oh Jezebel,
Let someone give me money!
Jezebel, oh Jezebel,
Bring lots of cash to me!'

Charles kicked a little soil over the wax ball to hide it, then glanced over to Earl. 'We gotta go,' he whispered, his eyes darting around the deserted cemetery as though he had seen something. 'Best hurry too,' he added, grabbing Earl by the arm and pulling him along. 'And whatever you do, don't look back, otherwise dead spirits'll catch your gaze and follow us home.' These words sent a cold shiver through Earl and he ran faster than he had ever run in his life.

'The upshot of that spell was incredible, and went far beyond mere money,' Earl recalled nearly ninety years later. 'I met a holy man who gave me money and took me across the sea. We visited the pyramids, the Holy Land and the Red Sea. He showed me the mysteries and places of power so that I could help people when I got back. We collected incense, charms and other magical items. Then the holy man said, "You are now a Prince among Hoodoos – use your power well."'

DOCTOR JOHN

According to Charles the Grinder, the Jezebel money charm was a favourite of Doctor John, the famed and flamboyant Voodooist who operated in New Orleans during the nineteenth century. Doctor John was a freeman of colour, who claimed to be a Senegalese prince. The grotesque scars covering his fierce face, he insisted, were proof of his royal descent, in that they were ceremonial marks put there by his father, a great king, following the tradition of their royal family. When the Spaniards

(Continued on page 36.)

Doctor John, the famed and flamboyant voodooist of nineteenth-century New Orleans.

⌐ LUCKY MONEY MOJO ⌐

You can also use a Voodoo or Lucky Mojo doll *(see page 46 for instructions on making Voodoo dolls)* to cast a money-drawing spell. First, set up your altar. Then burn some Money Drawing Incense and pass your doll through the smoke to consecrate it. Anoint a green candle with Money Oil, place it on a white saucer and light it. Using Dragon's Blood or Dove's Blood Ink, write out your request for money on a piece of parchment paper (your request could read along the lines of 'Spirits, bring me money to meet my needs'). Now put some coins inside the doll, along with a whole John the Conqueror root. Then sprinkle the doll with Money Drawing Powder and anoint it with bayberry oil. As you do this, recite the prayer below. Once the spell is cast, put the doll where you can always see it, and don't let anyone touch it. Every seven days, place one or two coins in front of the doll to feed it and rekindle its taste for money.

'Money doll, money doll,
Bring me riches, bring me gold,
Money doll, money doll,
Fill my bank full of cash.'

arrived in Senegal, however, Doctor John was sold into slavery. Eventually, by guile and cunning, he won his freedom. He then took to the high seas, travelling the world, working on sailing vessels. During this time he discovered his 'power', and decided to settle in New Orleans, where he set up as a Voodoo doctor, specializing in healing, selling gris-gris and telling fortunes.

By all accounts, Doctor John was an expert in money conjure and amassed a large fortune as a result. In his day, however, conjure work was often a good deal more macabre than it generally is today. When Doctor John performed the Jezebel spell, for example, instead of using plain white saucers as candle holders, he would have used human skulls, which had been stolen from graveyards throughout the city.

BUCKEYE CHARM

Even if conjure work fails to bring you the kind of affluence Doctor John enjoyed, it will get you out of financial scrapes. During the mid 1990s, I was down on my luck and couldn't afford to pay my telephone bill. I'd received warnings from the telephone company and fully expected to have the line cut off. In a final, desperate bid to make some cash, I decided to perform some gambling conjure, in the hope of getting a win on the national lottery.

A popular gambling charm amongst Hoodooists involves drilling a hole in a buckeye nut and filling it with quicksilver. This seemed the ideal charm to use. The way I figured it, buckeye nuts are very much the size and shape of male testicles. Therefore, from a homeopathic-magic point of view, the buckeye nut symbolizes the seed of life and growth – which fitted very nicely with my intention to sow the seeds of wealth and abundance in my life.

From a botanical perspective, the buckeye nut, which is reddish-brown in colour, is very similar to the horse chestnut, or 'conker', but is smaller and more spherical in shape. The buckeye tree, on which the nut grows, is native to North

America and is in fact a close relative of the horse-chestnut tree of Europe – so a conker would be a good replacement.

Although buckeyes are not readily available in the UK, where I was living at that time, I'd got some in my conjure bag, having picked them up from a botanica in L.A., during one of my regular business trips to the States. So I was all set to make up the charm.

Once I'd prepared my altar, I lit two green candles, and burnt some Gambler's Incense. Then I passed a buckeye nut through the incense smoke to consecrate it. I drilled a hole in the buckeye and poured some quicksilver into it. Taking some wax from one of the green candles, I proceeded to seal the hole. I then anointed the nut with Fast Luck Oil and then, using Dragon's Blood Ink, I wrote the verse at the bottom of the page on some parchment paper.

I put the parchment paper and buckeye nut in a green mojo bag, along with three silver coins. Once the spell was cast, I kept the buckeye charm bag in my pocket at all times.

Much of the magical reasoning behind this charm involves courting the influence of the Roman god Mercury, who rules over games of chance and sleight of hand. Quicksilver, being liquid mercury, is the central ingredient used for this purpose. In America, conjure workers also add a silver 'mercury' dime to the mojo bag to further increase the mercurial influence of the charm. Being resident in the UK, I simply substituted three silver coins for the dime. The general efficacy of the charm is increased by anointing the buckeye with Fast Luck Oil. If

'Buckeye nut,
Seed of wealth,
Bring gambling luck
To my own good self.'

To enhance the efficacy of the buckeye charm, add three silver coins to the mojo hand.

a buckeye cannot be obtained, then the charm is equally effective if you use a nutmeg or a whole John the Conqueror root.

One afternoon, a couple of days after making my buckeye charm, I fell asleep in an armchair and dreamt that I was filling out my lottery numbers. On coming round from the doze, the dream reminded me that I must get the form filled in ready for that evening. So I reached over to get it from the table next to me. To my astonishment, it had already been filled in – and I was 100 per cent certain that I hadn't done it previously. Could I have reached over and filled it in while I was asleep? Is such a thing possible? All I know for sure is the following Sunday, when I checked the newspaper, I found I had a modest win – £200, which was easily enough to cover my telephone bill. From then on my financial situation in general picked up and I had no further problems meeting bills.

LUCKY SANTEROS

In Cuba and in the United States many people wonder how those involved in the religion of Santeria, often very poor people, always seem to be able to afford the relatively high cost of initiations. The Kariocha initiation, for example, which makes a person a fully-fledged Santero (priest), can cost the equivalent of two years' wages for a low-income worker. Stories of people depriving themselves of all luxuries for years in order to pay for their initiations are common, but more perplexing are stories, also common, of people who pay for their initiations with money won in the lottery or other games of chance, supposedly after an Orisha (god or goddess) or a guardian spirit revealed to them which numbers to play. Santeros believe Orishas and guardian spirits have the ability to predict what number will come out in the lottery or what horse will win a race. However, spirits rarely give numbers in a direct manner; instead, they give coded clues that require special knowledge to interpret them.

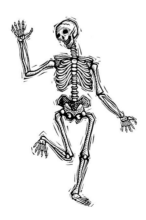

Chapter Three

WINNING LOVE

'Bring me a teaspoonful o' sugar, a small jar o' honey, and a leaf from a fig tree – and I give ya the woman, if that's what ya want.'

Saheed, a Southern States Conjure Man, 1970

inding a partner, soul-mate or simply a one-night stand using Voodoo has always been popular. Indeed, stories abound about how the lovelorn have won the love of the man or woman of their dreams using plants, potions and whispered enchantments under a Hoodoo moon.

MAMAN CELIE

William Seabrook, a writer who lived in Haiti during the 1920s, described how an old Voodoo priestess named Maman Celie made a love charm to ensure that her grandson, Paul, would be successful in winning the love of one Ti-Marie, a girl who, until then, had shunned him.

Maman Celie first ground up the dried body of a hummingbird in a mortar, then added some jungle-flower pollen and some drops of her grandson's blood and semen, while uttering the following chant: 'Wood of the woods, woman you were created by God. Bird of the woods, fly into her heart. I command you in the name of the three Marys and in Ayida's [a Voodoo deity] name. Dolor, Dolori, passa.' She also crooned incomprehensible incantations.

When all the ingredients were as fine as dust, Maman Celie transferred them to a leather pouch, made from the scrotum of a he-goat, and gave it to Paul. Seabrook was later told that the grandson threw Maman Celie's concoction full into Ti-Marie's face as she passed him. Apparently, she spat like a wildcat and cried that she would kill Paul – but within a few hours she had yielded to his advances.

Maman Celie,
high priestess of formidable power.

'Doubtless a deeper magic than Maman Celie's was also at work,' comments Seabrook in his book *Magic Island* (1929). 'But I think it would be a mistake to assume a priori that without Maman Celie's incantations and the humming bird, Ti-Marie would have yielded.'

MARIE LAVEAU

In New Orleans, the most famous of all the Voodoo queens was a woman named Marie Laveau, who plied her occult trade during the nineteenth century. Many of Laveau's clients sought help in affairs of the heart, and the 'Laveau ladies', as they were called, were never short of prescriptions. A favourite wile for a woman in love was to steal a glove from the man she was after, then fill it with sugar, honey and steel dust. To make the enchantment work, the lady had only to sleep with the glove under her mattress. A woman worried about a straying husband might mix a few drops of her menstrual blood in his dinner. Women who applied this curative to their men often referred to it as 'the Marie Laveau trick'.

If a woman passionately desired a married man, Marie would write the names of the man and his wife on a piece of paper and place it in an animal's bladder, then leave the bladder out in the sun to dry. The man, it was said, would soon leave his wife, and all his new flame had to do to keep him

Sugar and honey placed in a man's glove will sweeten his affections, and steel dust will strengthen your hold over him.

was regularly anoint herself with the various love powders and oils provided by Marie. Conversely, for parents who disapproved of the man courting their daughter, Marie would mix a favourite gris-gris (charm), the ingredients of which included gunpowder, dried mud from a wasp's nest, flaxseed, cayenne pepper, shotgun pellets, powdered sassafras, bluestone and Dragon's Blood. The parents were then instructed to toss the mixture on the steps of the undesirable suitor's house. This, asserted Marie, would ensure the suitor lost his ardour.

SEX CONJURE

The idea that you can bring love into your life by using spells, herbs and potions may seem far-fetched to some. Earl Marlowe, however, made no bones about it. 'Hoodoo love potions work,' he insisted, and recounted an instance of how as a young man he had used Hoodoo to bring love into his life.

At that time, Earl was living in Louisiana and had picked up a little Voodoo lore from the locals, which he blended with his own tradition of Trinidadian folk magic. This meant that his love spell was highly eclectic and individual. He engraved a silver talisman with a heart that had an erect penis stabbing through the middle of it. Earl explained that the heart denoted Erzulie, Voodoo goddess of love, while the penis denoted Legba, phallic god of fertility in Voodoo.

'When you bring these two powerful spirits together in a conjure working,' he said, 'it increases your animal magnetism a hundred fold and then it's only a matter of time before your every sexual fantasy is fulfilled.'

'So the spell was successful?' I asked.

'You could say that,' he grinned. 'Shortly after leaving the apartment where I worked the conjure, a girl – a complete stranger – just couldn't take her eyes off me, and this happened two or three times on the short walk to the nearby liquor store. But what was truly startling was that by that evening I had the option of sleeping with no less than nine different women ....'

THE OSHUN SPELL

Earl went on to describe a suitable love magic formula which he felt could be used to excellent effect by the average man or woman in the street.

'To prepare for what I call the Oshun spell,' he said, 'you would first need to cut photos from magazines of people who are generally considered to be attractive. If you're a man, people like Robert Redford or Tom Cruise; if you're a woman, Sharon Stone or Pamela Anderson. Study these photos; get behind the person's gaze and feel how it feels to be considered extremely attractive.'

Earl believed that by doing this you 'absorb' the power of your chosen celebrity, to the point that you almost become that person, and believe that you have as much sex appeal and charisma as the person you are focusing on.

'You do this for seven days,' continued Earl, 'and then perform the spell itself.'

This is best done when both hands on the clock are rising and the moon is waxing. First, set up your altar, do a cleansing ritual *(see page 20)* and burn suitable incense. Use Love and Attraction Oils – on your body or to anoint your candles, whatever feels right – and practise some candle magic *(see page 22)*. Finally, you invite Oshun, Santeria goddess of love, to overshadow you.'

Although Earl recommended this spell for the layman, he did give a word of warning. 'One thing you must remember is that with conjure you draw the good and the bad. It exposes the darkest depths of your psyche, and so if you do a sexually motivated love spell you'll certainly get sex, but you have to be prepared to meet and possibly end up having a pretty ugly scene with some screwballs.'

VOODOO-DOLL LOVE RITUAL

A traditional way of bringing romance into your life is to use a Voodoo doll. For this spell you will need two dolls. They can be bought *(see suppliers, page 125)*, but are simple and fun to make yourself *(see page 46)*.

An effective love ritual using Voodoo dolls can be performed as follows. (I will describe this from my own, masculine point-of-view, but it can easily be adapted for a woman to attract a man, or by either sex to attract the same sex.)

Firstly, you will need two Voodoo dolls: one to represent you, the other to represent the person you wish to enchant. Then set up your altar in the usual way. Appropriate incenses to burn would be Lovers Incense or Love Me Incense (patchouli). Now perform a purification ritual and anoint two red candles with Love Oil and Attraction Oil. (Remember that in works of attraction, you rub the oil from the wick to the base of the candles.) When this is done, using a new nail, write your name on one candle and the name of your intended lover on the other. Put them in brass candle holders side by side on the altar. Then put the doll that represents you in front of the candle with your name on, and the doll that represents your lover-to-be in front of the candle with her name on it. Now light the candles and say, 'May the light of love shine down on this man and this woman.'

TRANCE

Now get yourself into a deep trance. Stare at a candle … or at the swirling smoke of the incense …. Be aware of your peripheral vision … the walls … the window … and listen to sounds … cars outside … birds singing … and feel the different sensations in your body …. They are there all the time … but you don't normally notice them …. This is a good opportunity to be aware of your feet … your arms … your fingers …. As you do this you will feel more … and more … relaxed ….

LOVE RITE

Now pick up the dolls, one in each hand, and get them talking to each other. Do this out loud. The doll which represents you could say, 'Hi, we're in this magical world together. I don't know how we got here, but it is a beautiful place, and I couldn't think of anyone more wonderful to be with at this time than you ….'

(Continued on page 47.)

⌐ MAKING A VOODOO DOLL ⌐

Cut a human outline from two pieces of cloth (1) and sew them together, leaving a hole at the top of the head, so that the doll can be stuffed (2). The material used for stuffing the doll can be anything from cotton to straw, Spanish moss to herbs. However, an essential ingredient that should be mixed in with the stuffing material is a personal item taken from the person it is meant to represent: hair, nail-clippings, a fragment of clothing, blood, sexual fluids or saliva, are all ideal. However, care should be taken that these items are acquired without the person's knowledge.

Once the doll is sewn up, every effort must be made to ensure that it actually looks like the person it is meant to represent. For example, if the person has brown hair and dark eyes, then use brown wool for the doll's hair and dark thread for the eyes (3). When the doll is completed, it should be wrapped in a clean white linen cloth or in white tissue paper until it is needed.

(1)   (2)   (3)

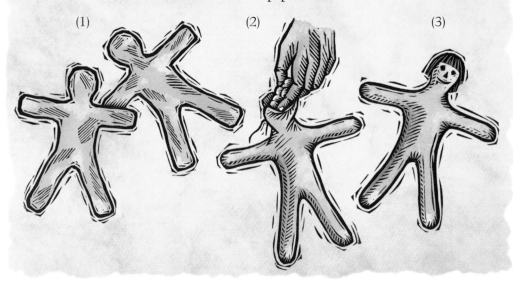

The doll representing your lover-to-be could reply, 'I feel the same. It's like I never really noticed you before, but now I've seen something special in you, something that makes you stand out from the crowd. I don't know what it is exactly; I mean I can't put my finger on it, but it is there all the same, like a light shining from you ….'

The dialogue should become more and more romantic and passionate, to the point that the dolls' hormones are literally singing with desire. You could then have them kiss each other tenderly … caressing each other … undressing each other … and then making love. Make the whole thing realistic. Verbalize their groans and moans of desire, and have them make love in different positions. Finally, when they both reach heaving, ecstatic climax, give a high-pitched yell for the female orgasm and a long, deep animalistic moan for the male. Once the two lovers are satiated, have them lie tenderly together, whispering 'sweet nothings' to each other.

Once you feel the love rite has come to a natural conclusion, give your thanks to the spirits and sprinkle some holy water around your working area. Then extinguish the black and white altar candles, but leave the red candles to (safely) burn down. You may also find it beneficial to 'earth' yourself by having a warm drink and something simple to eat. This will help you to forget all about the ritual, thus leaving the magic (or unconscious) forces in peace to set about bringing your romantic desires to fruition. The idea behind this spell is that you trust your unconscious, which, I can assure you, knows what is best for you. So long as your desires are congruous with your deeper needs, it will bring them into reality.

There are other ways to use a Lucky Mojo or Voodoo doll to attract a lover. You can set up your magic altar with appropriately romantic oils, candles, incenses and flowers. Then fill your charm bag or doll with herbs, roots and personal items from the individual you wish to attract, and recite a rhythmic love chant over the charm. After that, the bag or doll is hung around your neck or carried in a pocket, until the person you have enchanted becomes your lover.

TO BIND A LOVER TO YOU

Once you have a lover, you may wish to ensure that he or she never leaves you. A good ritual for this requires the following ingredients.

1 teaspoon of couch grass (chopped or ground)
1 bottle of Luv Luv Oil
1 packet of Love Powder
1 bottle of Love Oil
1 large red candle

First sprinkle the couch grass under your bed, on the mattress and under your pillows. Then, when you rise each morning, rub a little Luv Luv Oil on your genitals and sprinkle a little Love Powder over your pubic hairs. (Be careful using these ingredients on your body – test them on a small area of skin first.)

Anoint the candle with Love Oil. Then, using your own blood or Dove's Blood Ink, write your lover's name on parchment. Put the paper on a white saucer and the candle on top of it. Burn the candle every morning while you dress and extinguish it on leaving the room. Do this for seven days and your lover will never leave you.

SEDUCTION OIL

Here is the recipe for Seduction Oil. To add to the power of any love spell, wear this as a perfume on a daily basis. You will need the following ingredients.

2 tablespoons of cloves
50 ml (2 fl oz) of oil (virgin olive oil or good-quality vegetable oil)
Verbena root (said to make the passions rise)

(Continued on page 50.)

⁓ LOVE ATTRACTION CHARM ⁓

A powerful love attraction charm, reputedly devised by Marie Laveau, is easily prepared by carefully mixing the following ingredients.

½ teaspoon of archangel herb (angelica)
1 teaspoon of Lovers Incense
1 teaspoon of spearmint (chopped)

Take a piece of parchment paper and write your prospective lover's name on it seven times in either your own blood (women should use menstrual blood) or in Dove's Blood Ink (1). Now place the parchment paper, herbs and incense in an old tin can. Carefully set the contents alight and let them burn to ashes (2). When this is done, collect the cool ashes and put them into a red flannel (mojo) bag (3). Tightly tie the top of the bag and hang it around your neck on a white cotton string. This charm will render the one you love unable to resist making love to you – marriage may even be a possibility.

(1)   (2)   (3)

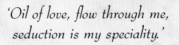

'Oil of love, flow through me,
seduction is my speciality.'

Crush the cloves into the oil using a pestle and mortar. Then bottle the mixture, adding a small piece of verbena root to each bottle you make. Store in a dark, previously consecrated place for seven days before using.

Anoint yourself daily, behind the ears, under the left armpit, on the back of the neck and between the thighs. As you do this, recite the chant above.

RABBIT & THE HERB DOCTOR

Many of these concoctions might seem a little convoluted, if not outright bizarre to some. But, believe me, they're nothing compared to the kind of ingredients that used to be used in love spells, long ago in Africa. One wonderful old tale, recorded on the cotton plantations of the southern states during the nineteenth century, illustrates this. It concerns Rabbit, the trickster – a character close to my heart and a familiar spirit I've had to call on many times during my life.

Long, long ago, Rabbit fell in love with a high-cheek-boned beauty, with long obsidian hair. In order to ensure his courtship went smoothly, he went to an African herb doctor for some love magic.

'Bring me an elephant tusk, an alligator tooth and the bill of a rice-bird,' instructed the herb doctor, 'and I'll make you up a charm bag.'

So Rabbit went off in search of an elephant. Once he'd found an elephant, however, he realized the task was going to be far from easy. So the wily bunny thought for a moment and came up with a cunning plan. 'Lotsa folks roundabout say you da strongest animal in the whole world,' he said to the elephant, 'but I bets you can't uproot that big pine tree, over yonder?'

Indignant, the elephant charged the tree with all its might and uprooted it in one. But in so doing, one of his tusks got stuck in the trunk of the tree. Quick as a flash, Rabbit pulled the tusk from the fallen tree and took it to the herb doctor. Next, Rabbit located an alligator. He suggested that the two of them should clear away the undergrowth and make a good road to the creek. The alligator liked the idea and began to sweep the ground with its tail, while Rabbit beat the bush with a cane. Accidentally on purpose, Rabbit hit the alligator with his cane, knocking out a tooth, which he promptly picked up and took to the herb doctor.

Finally, Rabbit found a rice-bird and asked if it could fly.

'Of course I can fly,' replied the rice-bird and, when the wind blew, it flew up in the air to prove it.

Rabbit congratulated the rice-bird on its flying prowess, but wondered whether the bird could fly somewhere where there was no wind, and suggested it try flying in a house. Once Rabbit had located a suitable house, the rice-bird, full of confidence, flew around inside. Without a moment's hesitation, sly old Rabbit shut the door, caught the bird, extracted its bill and took it to the herbalist.

True to his word, the herb doctor made Rabbit a charm bag out of the ingredients. It worked a treat – not long afterwards, Rabbit married his girl.

Chapter Four

THE DEVIL'S PACT

'If you want to learn how to play anything you want to play and learn how to make songs yourself, you take your guitar and you go to where ... a crossroad is .... A big black man will walk up there and take your guitar, and he'll tune it ....'

Tommy Johnson (1896–1956), celebrated bluesman

We were driving through the heart of the Mississippi Delta on a spiritual mission. We were trying to locate the holy of holies for Hoodoos – the crossroads where, sometime during 1930, the influential bluesman Robert Johnson allegedly sold his soul to the Devil in exchange for guitar expertise and fame. No one knows the exact location of Johnson's crossroads; so we were relying on instincts to find it.

Earl was at the wheel and I was riding shotgun in the big red Cadillac we'd hired back in Jackson. The midday sun burnt down on us.

'Do you believe Robert Johnson really sold his soul to the Devil?' I asked Earl.

'Yeah, I believe it,' he answered. 'You gotta believe it if you're black. It's the whites that don't believe it.'

Earl went on to explain that Johnson's biographers and commentators tend to fall into two racial camps: the black bluesmen who knew him and believe he made a pact with the Devil at the crossroads, and the white folklorists and musicologists, who don't. So far as Earl was concerned, Johnson's white biographers are university-educated intellectuals, full of pompous rationality. Accordingly, they describe him as an 'existential' blues singer, who died young and tragically, and compare him to white romantic figures such as Orpheus, John Keats and James Dean. Earl was utterly repelled by this.

'They paintin' a white face on a black man,' he insisted. 'Why, in the name of the Devil himself, don't they at least compare Johnson to Jimi Hendrix or Bob Marley?'

Earl argued that white authors tend to distort Johnson's story to the point that it reads more like a Shakespearean tragedy than what it really is – an odyssey into the world of Hoodoo. 'You wanna find the key to Robert Johnson, then study Hoodoo,' he stated. 'But there ain't many white intellectuals got the guts to do that.' In Earl's view, the Faustian pact mythos surrounding Robert Johnson simply reveals that he had been involved with a Hoodoo practitioner who taught him the mystical lore of the crossroads.

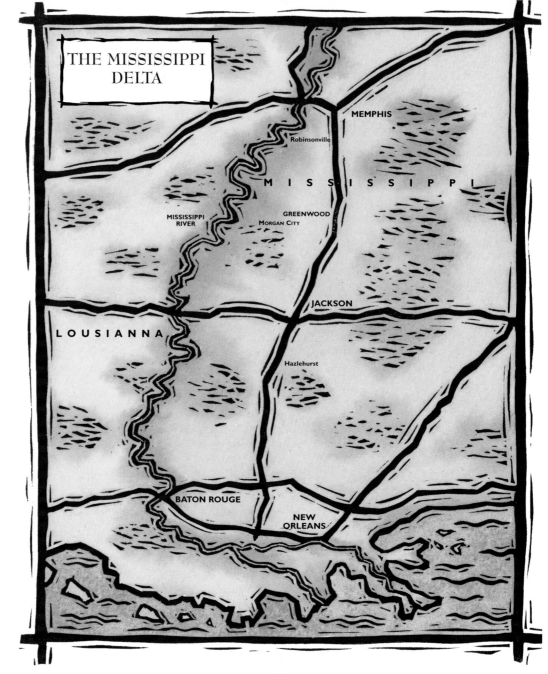

THE MISSISSIPPI
DELTA

MEMPHIS

Robinsonville

M I S S I S S I P P I

MISSISSIPPI
RIVER

GREENWOOD
MORGAN CITY

JACKSON

LOUSIANNA

Hazlehurst

BATON ROUGE

NEW
ORLEANS

THE MAN BEHIND THE MYTH

As we drove further down the dusty roads of Mississippi, we sank into silence, and I mused on Robert Johnson's life story – the facts of which are sketchy and vague. He was probably born on May 8, 1911, in Hazlehurst, Mississippi – the result of a brief extramarital affair between Julia Ann Dodds and a local plantation worker called Noel Johnson. Two years previously, Julia's husband Charlie had been run out of Hazlehurst by a lynch mob, due to falling out with some local landowners, called the Marchetti brothers. The Marchettis later also evicted Julia from her home, forcing her to send her children, including Robert, to live with Charlie, who had settled in Memphis, Tennessee, with his mistress and their two children. But around 1919, Robert returned to the Delta, to the area around Robinsonville, to live with his mother and her new husband, Dusty Willis. Robert is said to have taken on the name Johnson as a teenager when he learned who his real father was; up until then he'd been called Robert Leroy Dodds Spencer.

Music was a long-time interest for Johnson, and his first instruments were the Jew's harp and the harmonica. Before he became seriously involved with the guitar, however, he married Virginia Travis in February 1929, and the young couple soon became expectant parents. But tragedy struck when Virginia, only sixteen years old, died in childbirth in 1930.

Around June of that year, renowned blues musician Son House moved to Robinsonville. His music deeply affected Johnson, who considered it the 'rawest, most direct pure emotion' he had ever heard, and he followed House and his musical partner, Willie Brown, wherever they went. By this time he had dedicated himself to playing the guitar, but apparently didn't have much of a gift for the instrument. Commenting on his playing, Son House said, 'Such another racket you ever heard! It made people mad, you know. They'd come out and say, "Why don't y'all go in there and get that guitar from that boy! He's running people crazy with it."'

DELTA OF THE DAMNED

Unhappy and unwilling to be caught in the sharecropper's world of backbreaking work with little reward, Johnson left Robinsonville and headed deep into the Delta, to near Hazlehurst, his birthplace. There he played the jook joints, which were tumbledown shanties where people danced, drank, gambled and listened to music. He also found a 'kind and loving woman' more than ten years his senior, named Calletta 'Callie' Craft. The couple were married in May 1931, but, at Johnson's insistence, they kept the marriage a secret.

Johnson's time in southern Mississippi was very important because it was there that his musical talent came to fruition. When he returned to Robinsonville, Son House and Willie Brown were astounded by his development. 'He was so good!' recalled Son. 'When he finished, all our mouths were standing open. I said, "Well, ain't that fast! He's gone now!"' This was when rumours began about Johnson trading his soul to the Devil in exchange for guitar expertise. Not only had he suddenly become a brilliant musician, but he had also gained extraordinary charisma, to the point that his performance often moved a crowd to tears. He also attracted many blues players, destined to become famous in their own right, as his disciples. On top of all this, his career took off.

The idea that you could sell your soul to the Devil in exchange for talent and fame was not new; it had been a part of black culture for years. The Reverend LeDell Johnson (no relation to Robert)

Robert Johnson (1911–38) is reputed to have sold his soul to the Devil in exchange for guitar expertise and fame.

described how his brother Tommy, like Robert Johnson, left home scarcely able to play the guitar and came back an accomplished musician.

'Now, if Tom was living, he'd tell you. He said the reason he knowed so much, said he sold hisself to the Devil. I asked how. He said, "If you want to learn how to play anything you want to play and learn how to make songs yourself, you take your guitar and you go to where a road crosses that way, where a crossroad is. Get there, be sure to get there just a little 'fore twelve that night so you know you'll be there. You have your guitar and be playing a piece there by yourself …. A big black man will walk up there and take your guitar and he'll tune it. And then he'll play a piece and hand it back to you. That's the way I learned to play anything I want."'

Son House was convinced that Robert Johnson had done the same thing, as were many other blues players.

Johnson went to San Antonio late in November, 1936. There, over a period of five days, he made his first recording. When he was finished, he returned home to Mississippi. Being a recording artist brought Johnson a good degree of fame; he now found eager and expectant crowds nearly everywhere he played. Johnson travelled to such places as St. Louis, Memphis, Illinois, and back home to the Delta. Then, on Saturday night, August 13, 1938, at a jook joint named Three Forks, near Greenwood, Johnson played his last gig. Of the many rumours concerning Johnson's death, poisoning is the most substantiated. His death certificate was found in 1968, verifying that he died in Greenwood, Mississippi. He was buried in a small church in nearby Morgan City.

LEGACY

One of the few certainties about Robert Johnson's life and music is the lasting effect it has had on popular music and culture. Although not a household name himself, some of those who aspired to be like him are. Rock legends Jimmy Page

(Continued on page 59.)

⬩ CROSSROADS MAGIC ⬩

A central belief of Hoodoo, which has its roots in African sorcery, is the idea that the intersection of two roads, the crossroads, is a place of great magical power. According to one Hoodoo practitioner, a murderer can evade capture if he goes to a crossroads and takes nine steps backwards down the road opposite to that which he intends to travel along. This not only ensures that the law will always take the wrong road in their pursuit of the murderer, but also that their investigations will lead in directions other than his.

The crossroads is also the best place to dispose of the remnants of a job (or spell) – leftover candle wax, incense ashes, footprint dirt, ritual bath water, and so on. If you have worked a love spell, for example, then mark every crossroads between your home and the home of your prospective lover with ritual objects, to cement the bond and draw the desired one closer. In spells to drive away enemies, ritual items can be thrown into a series of crossroads on the way out of town, to push the hated person away and to act as deterrents against his or her return.

and Robert Plant (Led Zeppelin), Eric Clapton (Cream), The Rolling Stones and Elvis Presley, were all inspired by the music of Robert Johnson. And, in turn, their music has had an enormous impact on the development of pop, rock, country and blues – as well as on the styles of music that continue to derive from these forms. Rumour has it that Robert Plant keeps a vial of dirt, supposedly from Johnson's crossroads.

CROSSROADS RITE

At the very heart of blues and rock music, both of which have been described as the 'Devil's music', lies the shadow of the Faustian pact, as epitomized by Robert Johnson. But behind the mythos of the 'deal with the Devil' lies the Hoodoo lore of the crossroads. In Southern black communities during Robert Johnson's time, it was a commonly held notion that you could go to a crossroads and meet the Devil. This concept has its roots in the African belief that a guardian spirit inhabits the crossroads. The Yoruba tribes of Nigeria call this spirit Eshu, while the Fon of Dahomey call it Legba. This spirit is the intermediary not only between the supreme deity and the gods, but also between humans and the gods. This is why, in all African-derived religions worldwide, the crossroads deity is always first to be honoured and called upon in any ceremony.

The god of the crossroads is also a trickster. An unpredictable character, whose jokes and tricks are normally mischievous and benign, but do sometimes turn malicious. This aspect of the trickster is, no doubt, why the Christians, when they arrived in Africa, associated him with the Devil. The Africans who were taken to America as a result of the slave trade retained the demonic appellation, particularly in the southern states. But for them, the Devil wasn't the evil terror of Judeo-Christian belief. On the contrary, he was a tutelary spirit, who could teach you both physical and mental skills. Even his trickster nature served a teaching function in that it showed that being unpredictable and doing the unexpected were, in fact, creative and effective approaches to solving problems.

THE PRICE OF THE PACT

The tutelary aspect of the crossroads deity was emphasized by a friend of Earl's, the Reverend Gary Fox, a Texan conjure man, whom we visited before embarking on our odyssey into the Mississippi Delta.

'The Devil ain't nobody to be afeared of,' he insisted. 'He a spirit, like any other spirit. Ain't no better, ain't no worse. But if you want to learn how to do something – like how to play the guitar or banjo, or how to do sorcery, then you have to sell yourself to the Devil. That's the way it is.'

I asked him how one would go about this?

'You have to go to the cemetery at the stroke of midnight for nine nights, and get some dirt and bring it back with you and put it in a little bottle,' he replied. 'Then find a place where the roads cross, a crossroads, and at midnight, for nine nights, sit there and try to play that guitar. Don't care what you see come there, don't get 'fraid and run away.'

'What do people see?' I asked.

'Mostly they see black animals. Might be a black rooster, black bull, black dog or cat – even a black snake or lion. Usually, it's rainin' and a thunderin' too. Some say a black smoke comes down so's you can't see anything. Then, on the last midnight there will come a rider, in the form of the Devil, riding at lightnin' speed. You stay there, still playin' your guitar, and when he has passed, you can play any tune you want to play or do any magic trick you want because you have sold yourself to the Devil.'

So, from what the Rev. Gary Fox said, it would seem that selling your soul to the Devil doesn't have particularly dire implications. The myth surrounding Robert Johnson implies that, in exchange for fame and guitar brilliance, or whatever skill you are seeking, you must die young, forfeit your soul and spend eternity in Hell. But this isn't borne out by the evidence, as reported by actual Hoodoo practitioners.

I was beginning to wonder whether the Hoodoo notion of selling your soul to the Devil is more a metaphor than a real pact. It may describe the process of contacting our unconscious mind, which is the instinctive and creative aspect of ourselves. When you go to the crossroads, you learn to enter trance and thus, in effect, allow your unconscious mind – your 'Devil', perhaps – to come to the fore.

My take on what happened to Robert Johnson is that he went to a lonely crossroads, played some guitar and experienced visions on a par with those experienced by shamans during their initiatory vision quest. This allowed his unconscious, or inner-genius, to take control of his guitar playing – thus his musicianship became outstanding. It also brought him a high level of charisma – which is something you can learn to exude through profound contact with your unconscious resources. *(Continued on page 63.)*

⚊ FAME & FORTUNE RITE ⚊

If you are a musician, actor, artist or dancer and wish to achieve fame and fortune, then this rite will help you achieve your dreams. You must visit a lonely and desolate crossroads every night for seven nights. On the first day, clap your hands three times and call to the spirits of the place. Say something along the lines of the following chant.

> *'Spirits of the crossroads, show yourselves,*
> *Let us walk the lonely mile together,*
> *And let us share the dream of the Hidden God,*
> *Who lies deep within my being.'*

On the following five days, just go to the crossroads and talk with the spirits; tell them all about your artistic ambitions. Go into great detail, to the point of mapping out the level of success you would like to achieve over the next decade. On the seventh night, visit the crossroads at midnight, taking with you your musical instrument, paints or whatever you need. Acknowledge the spirits, then gather a few handfuls of crossroads dirt and rub it all over your face and body and in your hair. Then either play your musical instrument, act out a role, paint a picture or dance — whatever your chosen field. Once you get thoroughly engrossed, the spirits will possess you, body and soul. This might last for up to an hour. Once the spirits are gone, they will have left you with the gift of genius and you will go on to achieve great success with your chosen art. Remember to thank the spirits for their help and leave an offering of food or alcohol.

None of this is to say that the Devil, or the spirit of the crossroads, did not appear to Robert Johnson. It all depends on what model of reality you're using. If you believe in the Devil, as Johnson and other bluesmen did, then the Devil will appear. If you believe in the unconscious, then the unconscious will manifest itself. What matters is the results you get.

SNAKEMAN'S BLUES

By sundown, Earl and I had found what we instinctively felt was the crossroads where Robert Johnson sold his soul to the Devil. We parked up the Cadillac and sat down in the centre of the dusty crossing of the ways. I set up my guitar and began to play a slow, haunting blues. Earl blew a delicate tune on his harmonica to go along with it, then he gently sang a lyric I'd written. After we'd had something to eat, we pulled out our sleeping bags and went to sleep beside Robert Johnson's crossroads, under the Delta stars.

Chapter Five

HEALING HOODOO

'Sour, hour, vinegar-V!
Keep the sickness off of me!'

Voodoo 'vinegar' charm, quoted in the New Orleans newspaper *Times-Picayune*,
October 20, 1918

Afro-American folk medicine divides illnesses into three categories: those that are natural in origin, those caused by occult powers, and those that are spiritual in origin. The first group we will look at here are natural illnesses.

NATURAL ILLNESSES

Natural illnesses are brought about by the weather, cold air, damp and similar natural forces. These illnesses are cured with roots, herbs, barks, flowers and teas. All conjure workers are skilled in the use of therapeutic substances such as these. Indeed, herbal remedies have always played an integral role in the treatment of disease. In the past, of course, this was because orthodox medical treatment simply was not available to Afro-Americans; but even today traditional medicine is regularly used by those who do not trust conventional doctors and consider traditional remedies to be more effective. Many people involved in the practice of New World religions and magic hold this view.

In general, natural illnesses can be cured without the use of magic. Although, I would always recommend reciting a simple incantation over your preparation before you consume it or administer it to a patient. It would take a whole book to describe all the herbal remedies I use to treat my family, my clients and myself, but here are just a few which I use against common ailments.

COUGH AND COLD REMEDY

To cure coughs, colds and other respiratory ailments, eat a whole raw clove of garlic four to five times a day. To make it slightly more palatable, grind the clove into a pulp in a pestle and mortar, then scoop it up on a spoon and swallow it. It must be admitted that this treatment is thoroughly unpleasant; but it will get rid

of coughs and colds very quickly, often within 12–18 hours. Obviously, you have to be prepared for the fact that your breath, and indeed your whole body, will reek of garlic. But once you are well again, and have had a bath and brushed your teeth, the smell will have gone.

POMEGRANATE TONIC

An excellent tonic, well known in the American south, is made up with the following ingredients.

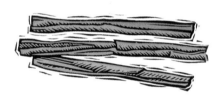

2 pints (1 litre) of wine
3 pinches of raw rice
1 heaped teaspoon of cinnamon
5 small pieces (about the size of a fingernail)
of the hull of a pomegranate
5 tablespoons of sugar

Put all the ingredients in a pan and let it slowly come to the boil. Take it off the heat, leave for half an hour to set, then strain. Take one tablespoon a day. This should keep for 3–4 days in the fridge. When pomegranate is in season, it is well worth gathering all the hulls you can for use at other times of the year.

MARIGOLD TONIC

Another excellent tonic is made from an infusion of marigold, rosemary and sundew *(Drosera rotundifolia)*. The effect is much enhanced by the addition of rock-rose (*Helianthemum*), a plant noted for its antidepressant qualities. It suits all age groups, including young infants.

½ quart (1 pint or ½ litre) of boiling water
1 oz (30 g) of dried herbs (or three handfuls
of the fresh herbs)

Pour the boiling water over the herbs, cover, then leave for 3–4 hours. Finally, strain the mixture into a bottle (if stored in a refrigerator, it will keep fresh for up to 4 days). Drink 1–3 wineglassfuls daily.

TO CALM THE NERVES

Drink a decoction of valerian root to quiet the nerves. Valerian has a relaxing and even euphoric effect on the system; its great value is that it calms the mind without having a narcotic effect. Its name is derived from the Latin, 'valeo', meaning, 'I am well'. You will need the following to make up the decoction.

½ oz (15 g) of dried valerian root
1 pint (½ litre) of water

Simmer the valerian root in the water for as long as it takes to reduce the water by half (usually some 20 minutes). The liquid should then be strained off into a bottle. It will keep for up to four days if kept in the refrigerator. Take one tablespoon of the mixture daily for one week, maybe two, but no more.

Cats become frisky on smelling valerian root; they roll on their backs in apparent ecstasy, much as they do at the scent of the herb catnip. Horses, too, are known to like its scent, as are rats and mice (in fact, it was once used as a bait in traps). Humans, however, find the smell of valerian root abhorrent, often comparing it to the stench of sweaty socks!

HEAL-ALL SPELL

You can also use conjure to cure natural illnesses. Here's an all-round curative spell, which I've regularly made good use of with clients. It is simple to do and requires only a few items, as listed below. *(See page 46 for details on making your own Voodoo doll.)*

Dragon's Blood Ink
Parchment paper
Voodoo doll
Healing Oil
White cloth
2 white candles

First perform an opening ritual, cleansing your working area with holy water. Then, using Dragon's Blood Ink, write the name of the person who needs healing on parchment paper. Now anoint the doll with Healing Oil, placing a few drops on the area of the doll corresponding to where the sick person is affected (1).

'Spirits of light, charge this doll,
with the power to heal, the power to cure;
so it will make [name]
fit and well and full of health'

Then recite the incantation *(opposite)* to gain the help of the healing spirits.

When I do these kind of chants, I don't necessarily stick to specific words. Usually I drift off into an unintelligible rhythmic chant – known to Hoodoo doctors as the 'unknown tongue'. I always keep the intent of the ritual focused clearly in my mind's eye, but I relinquish conscious control of my voice. This allows my unconscious mind, the powerhouse within, to come to the fore and speak in whatever way it chooses. Usually what comes out is completely abstract and incomprehensible to human ears, but is fully understood by the spirits; for it is their language – the tongue of angels, demons and fairies.

Once you have finished your chant, wrap the doll and parchment paper in the white cloth and place between the two white candles (2). Burn the candles each morning (replacing them as necessary) until the patient has made a full recovery. At that point, you can dispose of the doll. You should also make a point of thanking the spirits for their help. You could leave them an offering of some kind – fruit, herbs, liquor, milk or whatever seems appropriate (use your intuition in this matter).

(1)   (2)

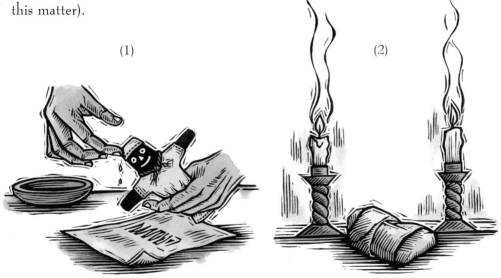

➤ DOCTOR YAH YAH'S VIOLET CHARM ➤

Violets were said by nineteenth century New Orleans Voodooist, Doctor Yah Yah, to be an excellent aid for avoiding or overcoming any illness or disease. He believed that these pretty purple flowers give off powerful healing vibrations. To gain the benefit of these vibrations, place some violets in a red flannel bag, tie the top shut, attach a cotton string and wear the bag around your neck for protection. Change the flowers in the bag every seven weeks. For even more potency, sprinkle some crushed violets in each corner of every room in your home.

Doctor Yah Yah violated the tradition that all Voodoo leaders were free, for he was a slave, whose real name was George Washington. His talents included fortune telling and healing. His career came to a sudden end in 1861, however, when he was jailed for selling poison to an Italian fruit dealer, who had taken the potion to a chemist before accepting it as a cure for his rheumatism. Doctor Yah Yah's master paid a fine to obtain his release and then shipped him off to end his days toiling as a field hand on a plantation.

HEALING POWER OF SANTERIA

All priests and priestesses of Santeria (known respectively as 'santeros' and 'santeras') are herbalists, and some possess a truly profound knowledge of the medicinal qualities of plants. Anyone even peripherally involved with Santeria knows about or will have heard of a seemingly miraculous cure effected by a santero or santera after conventional medical science had given up. Santeria, however, does not reject science; a santera or santero will sometimes recommend seeing a doctor for an operation or other conventional treatment, first preparing the patient with a magical herbal infusion, known as 'omiero'. Sometimes, however, a Santeria cure can make major interventions like surgery unnecessary. For example, while hosting a radio talk show in 1984, santero and writer Raul Canizares, suddenly lost his voice; talking became excruciatingly painful. 'A throat specialist told me I needed an emergency operation,' he recalls in his book *Cuban Santeria*, 'but my mother (a priestess of Santeria) made an infusion of some common weeds she called "romerillo". After gargling with the infusion for a few days, my voice was back to normal.'

OCCULT ILLNESSES

The individual suffering from an illness caused by occult powers has been cursed or hexed. They will frequently exhibit both behavioural and physical symptoms; perhaps behaving in an odd, eccentric or even 'insane' manner, as well as complaining of stomach or head pains. A hex need not result in physical symptoms, however. It may produce a run of bad luck, loss of a job or a strong desire to leave town. A person who has been hexed or cursed will not recover fully until the spell has been removed by a Hoodoo worker or conjuror.

KILLING THE ROOT

Illnesses caused by occult powers can be tricky to deal with. But, with a little ingenuity, most can usually be sorted out – as the following story involving Ed McTeer, High Sheriff of Beaufort County, South Carolina, from 1926–63, reveals. Besides being a white law enforcer, Ed McTeer was also a witch doctor. He had studied Hoodoo and African religion back in the late 1920s, in order to learn the ways of the local Afro-Americans, whom he regularly came into contact with during the course of his work. The following is one of his first conjure-related cases.

Prominent Beaufort farmer, Hal R. Pollitzer, told McTeer of a middle-aged woman living near his farm who was convinced that a root (curse) had been put on her. Several things had gone wrong in a short period, and she took these to be signs of a spell against her. She was now lying in bed, staring at the ceiling and refusing to talk or eat.

Hal suggested that McTeer arrest the root doctor who was responsible, but McTeer pointed out that they couldn't be sure that a root was involved. The poor woman could even have 'hexed' herself in trying to find a good explanation for her collection of woes.

In the end, McTeer agreed to go to the woman's house to see if he could be of assistance. When they arrived, they found the emaciated woman lying motionless in bed and staring at the ceiling. It was clear that something had to be done quickly, so McTeer launched into his conjure spiel.

'Someone has put a strong root on this woman, Hal,' he said, standing at the foot of her bed. 'I can feel it all around me! Hal, this woman can be saved, but only if you're willing

Sheriff Ed McTeer earned himself a reputation as a powerful conjure man.

to spend a large sum of money. This spell is too strong for me to handle alone; I'll have to hire Dr Hawk to help me find the root!'

'I don't care what it costs,' Hal answered, seeing that McTeer was getting through to the sick woman. 'Hire Dr Hawk!'

The reason McTeer chose Dr Hawk was that the woman believed her root had been put on by Dr Buzzard, and 'Hawk' sounded a fierce opponent to 'Buzzard'.

That night McTeer visited Dr Hawk. When he had explained the situation, Dr Hawk said that he'd help, and began to prepare a 'red root'. When it was finished, the two drove out to the woman's house at night and Dr Hawk buried the root at the foot of her front steps. The two then drove back to town.

The next morning McTeer picked up Dr Hawk and they drove out to the house to find a large crowd assembled outside to watch the 'doctors' at work. Even the sick woman had been wheeled, bed and all, to the open doorway.

As they'd prearranged, Dr Hawk stayed in the car, staring straight ahead, and McTeer walked towards the porch, where he began his act.

'Some terrible person has put a death root on this good woman, and Mr Pollitzer has given me a large sum of money to hire Dr Hawk so that we can find the root and destroy it. Dr Hawk stayed up all night in the graveyard talking with the spirits, and he tells me that now he's ready to save this woman.'

With that, McTeer marched over to the car door and pulled it open. Dr Hawk stepped out and, rising to his full height, roared, 'Stand back! Stand clear of this house or you will all be sick!'

The crowd fell back. And as soon as they had cleared his way, Dr Hawk pulled out a knife and cut a long switch off a nearby tree. Bending it back and forth like a spring, he began to talk in the 'unknown tongue'. He walked up and down with his divining-root switch and, the moment he saw the sick woman rise up to get a better look, he let his voice reach a crescendo, and the switch flew from his hand to point at the exact spot where the red root had been planted the night before.

Dr Hawk went down on his knees, digging furiously. He found the root, tore it from its hiding place and held it over his head. At this the sick woman sat bolt upright in bed, and the crowd broke and fled in all directions at once.

'Stand clear!' Dr Hawk roared. 'This is a death root!' With that, he dashed off to the nearby river and threw the little red bundle far out into the water. When he returned he told the woman to sit up in bed, which she did with no trouble.

'Daughter, I have taken this terrible root off you,' he said. 'I have killed it and now you will get well. Eat and get your strength back.'

When McTeer returned to the house the following week, he found that the woman had made a miraculous recovery: she was up and about, eating, cleaning and cooking as usual. Had McTeer and Dr Hawk not intervened, however, it is likely she would have died – such was her belief in the power of Hoodoo.

DIVINING A HEX

If there is any doubt whether or not a trick (hex) has been laid, American root doctors sometimes place a dime under the client's tongue. If the client is under a spell of some kind, the dime turns black. I usually use a pendulum (known as a 'jack ball'), to ascertain this. I made my own pendulum from a small piece of oak. I shaved off the bark, sanded it down and rubbed boiled linseed oil into it. Finally, I drilled a hole through the middle and threaded a leather cord through it. But a jack ball can also be simply a mojo bag – serious practitioners would fill the charm bag with herbs and roots appropriate to divining.

First sort out a 'yes' and 'no' code by asking the pendulum a question to which there can only be one answer. For instance, if it is a bright summer's day, I might simply ask, 'Is the sun shining?' The pendulum will then begin to either oscillate to and fro or gyrate in a circle. Whichever response it makes, I take as the signal for 'yes'. I then hold the pendulum over the client and ask whether his or her illness is caused by a trick (malevolent spell). If the answer is affirmative, and if I feel sure the severity of the hex is minimal, I recommend they perform the following 'uncrossing' spell. Readers who believe they may be suffering from a hex-related illness or run of misfortune, may like to try it too.

UNCROSSING SPELL

First perform a standard opening ritual. Then you will need the following ingredients.

Rosemary oil
Some rainwater
Uncrossing Oil
Uncrossing Bath
Jinx Removing Bath
Uncrossing Powder

Put 7 drops of rosemary oil in a glass of rainwater. Stir in 9 drops of Uncrossing Oil and blend thoroughly, repeating the chant below. Then place the mixture in a window for three days. On the fourth day, sprinkle the water in all corners of your home – making sure no one can see you doing it.

Once you have done this, take a bath every day for seven consecutive days, adding 1 teaspoon of Uncrossing Bath and 1 teaspoon of Jinx Removing Bath to the water. When you have dried yourself off, rub Uncrossing Oil all over your body. As an extra measure, sprinkle a little Uncrossing Powder in your socks and shoes.

'Break the hex, blast the root,
free my life from the evil curse.'

SPIRITUAL ILLNESSES

Illnesses caused by a combination of negative mental attitude and unbalanced lifestyle fall within the category of spiritual illnesses. Like the forces of the occult, spiritual sources can produce misfortune as well as physical illness. Thus, illness, poor family relations, lack of a job and bad luck – frequently occurring together – can result from spiritual poverty. Illnesses that have a spiritual cause are best sorted out by either laying on hands and channelling healing energy into the sufferer, or by performing a blessing ceremony.

When I lay on hands, I visualize white light streaming down from above into my head, flowing through my body and entering the patient through my hands. As I perform this, I go into a trance state and utter the unknown tongues which, in this instance, are used to enlist the help of the various healing spirits with whom I am in spiritual contact. My intuition tells me when the person has been healed.

For the blessing ceremony, I first do an opening ritual to cleanse the working area of any unwanted psychic influences. Then I sprinkle the client with Holy Water and anoint their temples with Blessing Oil, while reciting a short prayer along the lines of the chant at the foot of this page.

Readers following this basic outline should have little problem relieving cases of spiritual depletion, characterized by negative mental attitude and unbalanced lifestyle.

'Spirits of healing, bring blessings upon [name],
may wealth, health and good fortune be forever his/hers.'

~ ADDICTION ~

Addictions are often the result of some kind of spiritual imbalance. But you first need to effect a swift cure of the symptoms before you can set about sorting out the spiritual causes that lie behind the addiction.

To cure a drug addict, go to the grave of a deceased loved one of the addict and rap with your knuckles on the headstone. This will wake up the spirit. Holding the headstone, call out to the spirit to help the drug addict reform and to kill his or her desire for drugs. To cure an alcoholic, go to a graveyard with two pieces of board. Using a pointed instrument, mark out in the dirt or grass a grave for the alcoholic. Call out to the spirits to make the alcoholic stop drinking and, as you do so, use a mallet to pound one piece of board into the head of the mock grave and one at the foot. Pound vigorously and keep calling to the spirits. If your calls become incomprehensible, so much the better, as the unknown tongue is the language the spirits understand.

These two spells were taught to me by my Hoodoo mentor, Earl Marlowe. They are interesting in that they reveal the tenacity of the original West African belief from which they are derived – namely that the spirits of ancestors can influence life in the temporal world.

Chapter Six

THE EVIL EYE

'I have cunyun jacks and mojo hands of all types and kinds.
I can give you graveyard dirt that make
hounds from hell chase dey tails.
I can turn de evil eye of a jealous husband ....'

Speech by 'Doc Cyclone', from *Rhythm Oil* by Stanley Booth

One winter evening, back in the late 1980s, Earl Marlowe and I were discussing business over a beer in The King's Head pub in Islington, north London, our regular drinking haunt. It was fairly busy with after-work drinkers, some of whom gave us curious glances. We tended to attract attention as Earl often wore bright and colourful African robes, along with purple-tinted sunglasses, the badge of a Voodoo doctor.

Then suddenly Earl put his glass of beer down on a mat. 'See that girl over there,' he said, nodding in the direction of an attractive young blonde sitting in the corner of the bar, with a group of friends. 'What do you notice about her?'

'Well, she's very attractive, outgoing, popular' I replied.

Earl shook his head. 'That's not what I mean,' he said. 'What you haven't noticed is that that girl has the evil eye.'

'The evil eye?'

'Yeah. The glance of doom. She doesn't even know she's got it, but she'll bring bad luck or illness on anyone, soon as look at them.' With that Earl made a strange hand gesture in the general direction of the girl. The gesture involved sticking out the index and little fingers of his right hand, while bending back the second and third fingers against the palm, under the thumb. He made me follow suit. 'That will avert any chance of the evil eye affecting us,' he explained.

I was somewhat sceptical about all this. After all, the girl looked pleasant enough and was clearly popular. If she really brought bad luck on people, then surely she wouldn't have any friends. I pointed this out to Earl.

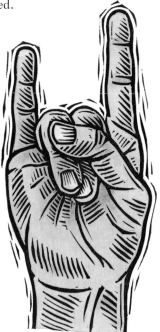

Two-horned hand gesture to avert the baleful influence of the evil eye.

He responded by telling me that the nineteenth-century Pope Pius IX was reputed to have wielded the evil eye.

'Like that girl over there, he had no idea of the power he had,' Earl added. 'And he was well loved, despite the fact that everything he touched turned bad. He blessed the Italian campaign against Austria in 1848, and straight away they lost battles. He blessed a new column to the Madonna and its workmen; and that very day a workman fell from the scaffolding and died. And so on. Nobody blamed the Pope; it wasn't his fault, but precautions against his gaze were necessary. When devout Catholics asked for blessing, they used to mutter a charm under their breath and do a hand sign, very much like you and I did just now. That way they deflected the blight of his eye.'

I was still sceptical. 'Do you really expect me to believe that people can bring bad luck or illness on others just by looking at them?' I asked.

'I do,' replied Earl. He then related an incident which occurred when he was in the merchant navy, some 30 years previously.

HIGH-SEA HEXES

'We were sailing around the coast of Madagascar, in the Indian Ocean,' he began. 'From the moment we set out on that particular voyage, things just kept going wrong. Usually it was only minor things, but they all added up. Then things took a turn for the worse. We were struck by a severe storm; it came out of nowhere, no warning. One minute the skies were clear and the sea was calm, the next, wham – tremendous storm hit. And I'll tell you, we were lucky to get out of that one alive. A few days afterwards, one of the men went overboard, during a dead calm. When we fished him out, he said he couldn't understand what had happened. He said it felt like something had compelled him overboard.' Apparently he was never the same after this. He kept gibbering about there being an 'evil influence' on board.

Because of this, a couple of seamen asked Earl if he thought there might be some curse or jinx involved. He said it was a possibility and that he'd look into it. 'I spent some time wandering around on deck,' he recalled. 'And I noticed this seaman, a white guy. There was something about him; he had hypnotic eyes, kind of stared at people too long. One time I caught him staring at the captain of the ship. Not long afterwards the captain fell sick with a high fever. That clinched it for me; I knew the guy had the evil eye. But I was also sure that he was unaware of the power he wielded. He was a genuinely nice guy. But every time I went near him or spoke to him I'd do the two-horned hand gesture to avert any risk of the evil eye affecting me. In the end, the other seamen began to notice the way he stared at people and they started to blame him for the string of misfortunes. It got to the point where they were talking of throwing him overboard. I told them that it needn't come to that and that I'd put things right. I then went down to my cabin and worked some serious conjure to put a stop to the curse of the evil eye – at least for as long as the voyage lasted.'

EVIL EYE ELIMINATOR

According to Earl, the spell he used on board ship to avert the evil eye can be used to good effect by anyone believing they are under the baleful influence of the eye of doom. The spell is known as the 'Evil Eye Eliminator' and these are the items you will need to execute it.

2 black candles
Repelling Incense
Reversible skull candle
Repelling Oil
A large bunch of bananas
Black ribbon

'Evil eye, turn your gaze away from me,
Look, instead, into the mirror,
And let your evil be returned to sender.'

As usual, perform a cleansing ritual, then light the black candles and burn some Repelling Incense. Take the reversible skull candle (these candles are used for dispelling evil and for cleansing) and rub it thoroughly with Repelling Oil, while uttering the chant above.

Now place the skull candle in an unobtrusive place in your home. High up on a shelf out of the way would be ideal. Once you have done this, return to your altar and pass the bunch of bananas through the Repelling Incense smoke. Next tie the black ribbon around the bananas and hang them outside from the roof of your house until they go rotten. They will absorb any residue of the evil eye that may still be lurking in your home. When the bananas are completely rotten, take them to a crossroads and bury them, speaking the Hoodoo doctors' unknown tongues. If you're at sea, do what Earl did, and simply throw them overboard.

A WORLDWIDE BELIEF

After leaving The King's Head, I set about doing some research into the evil eye. Going through my extensive collection of reference books, I discovered that the power of the eye to cast a spell or curse is among the oldest and most common beliefs in the world. In ancient times it was thought that the eye exerted a beam and that evil-minded people could manipulate and intensify their eye-beams to wreak havoc and harm. References to the evil eye can be found in the annals of the ancient Sumerians, Egyptians and Babylonians, as well as in Greek and Roman mythology. The evil eye is even mentioned in the Bible. In the King James version, the Book of Proverbs counsels, 'Eat though not the bread of him that hath an evil eye …. The morsel which thou hast eaten shalt thou vomit up.'

The evil eye was particularly feared in Naples – even in the twentieth century – where people shunned the owner of the evil eye, called the 'Jettatore'. Whenever he or she approached, the streets would clear of men, women and children. In Greece, Turkey, India and China it was believed that the evil eye had the power to harm horses and cattle, while in Britain the evil eye was reckoned to be cast by farmers on their rivals to harm crops.

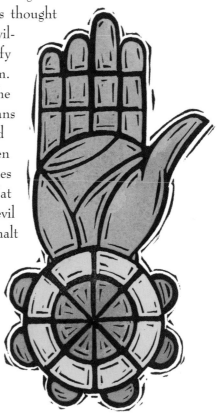

The Hand of Fatima is a very famous amulet, of Arab origin, against the evil eye. Fatima, the daughter of the prophet Mohammed, was a woman of great virtue.

⚊ CROSSBONES AMULET ⚊

One of the most powerful charms you can carry against the evil eye is the Crossbones amulet. To make one, you will need the following items.

(1)

Drive Away Evil Incense
1 white candle
Power Oil
Black thread
2 small bones taken from chicken wings

Set up your altar in the usual manner, this time burning Drive Away Evil Incense. Pass the white candle through the incense (1), then dress it with Power Oil (rubbing away from you). Now place the candle in a holder and light it. Using the black thread, tie the chicken bones together so they form an equal-armed cross (2). As you do this, recite the chant below. When the crossbones amulet is completed, sprinkle it with holy water. Wear it on a leather cord around your neck anytime you think you may be under threat from the evil eye.

'Crossbones, deflect the evil eye,
Let no negativity get to me;
Protect me from the envy of others,
And from their malicious glare.
Crossbones, swallow up the baleful glance,
And spit it back into the sender's face.'

(2)

Though not as prevalent today as in the past, belief in the evil eye is still strong in many areas of the world, including parts of Asia, Northern Africa, Southern Europe and in all areas of the New World where Santeria, Voodoo or Hoodoo is practised. In Africa the evil eye is believed to be inherited; those born with it cannot remove it. Allegedly, it can cause abortion, make spears break, make rats eat the corn or sicken cows. As in other parts of the world, the only way to counteract the curse that can kill at a glance is by using charms and hand gestures.

The use of the evil eye – sometimes called 'overlooking' – is most commonly thought to be motivated by envy. If you win the lottery or achieve success of one sort or another then, unbeknown to you, friends or neighbours could well exert the evil eye against you – despite themselves in many cases. Jealous lovers can pose a serious threat in this respect too; Hoodoo doctors are forever sorting out problems resulting from the malicious glance of a spurned husband or wife, or boyfriend or girlfriend. The supposed effects of the evil eye can assume a myriad of forms, ranging from financial troubles and long runs of bad luck, to headaches, sudden fatigue, accidents, illness and even death.

FEAR AND LOATHING IN THE SUBURBS

Although my researches showed that belief in the power of the eye to cause harm is widespread and, accordingly, there could be a grain of truth in the idea, I still remained sceptical. But then events led me to change my mind. I literally walked right into the midst of an incident of the evil eye.

During the early 1990s, a colleague of mine, who I'll call Vanessa, telephoned me early one evening and asked me to call round. As I had little on that evening, I was able to go round to her house more or less straight away. It turned out that Vanessa was feeling guilty about having cast the evil eye on her two immediate neighbours.

One was a young man called Ricky, who lived with his parents. He had a 'hot-hatchback' car and three or four times a week would return home late at night, having been to a nightclub. This was not a problem in itself; it was just that he persisted in slamming his car door when he got home, which woke Vanessa up. The other neighbour, Al, was a bachelor in his mid-fifties. Although extremely quiet most of the time, at weekends he would take his cassette player out into the garden and play old-time music-hall tunes very loudly. To Vanessa, this was too much. Although she was outwardly pleasant to both these neighbours, she was secretly giving them the withering glance of the evil eye.

Just as she had finished telling me all this, there was a loud knock at her door. It was Al, her bachelor neighbour. 'Someone's put petrol in the alley next to my house and my fence is on fire,' he exclaimed. I immediately jumped up and went to help Al. Between us, we easily put the fire out. He then told me how that evening had been a nightmare for him. He had been outside sweeping fallen leaves from his drive when he noticed a strong smell of petrol, which seemed to be coming from the alley next to his house. He went to investigate and found a pool of petrol a couple of yards down the alley. Not far away was a teenage boy, so Al went over to him to see if he knew anything about the petrol.

Al made the mistake of saying, 'Come here kid, I want to show you something.' Unsurprisingly, the teenager ran away. Al shrugged and went back to his house to try and find some rags to mop up the petrol. Once he'd found some, and was about to make his way back to the alley, a car screeched up behind him. Out got the teenage boy along with three burly youths.

'That's him!' exclaimed the boy. The three youths promptly leaped on Al.

Luckily, before he got too badly hurt, Al managed to explain himself and they saw reason. The next thing, however, was that whoever had poured the petrol in the alley had now set it on fire.

After I'd helped Al put out the fire, I walked back towards Vanessa's house. At that very moment, Ricky, Vanessa's other neighbour, climbed into his hot hatchback, gunned the engine and … bang! The engine blew up. Seconds later, his head was under the bonnet surveying the extent of the damage. I joined him. 'Oh, no,' he said, 'It's had it. It's a write off.'

I went back to Vanessa's house. 'This evil eye business has got to stop,' I said. 'Keep it up and you run the risk of killing people.' I returned the next day to perform a blessing ritual to nullify the effects of her evil glance. Despite chastising her, I couldn't help but be impressed by the results she had achieved using the evil eye.

BANISHING THE EVIL EYE

If you have suspicions that someone is casting the evil eye on you, then there is a way of discovering for certain whether this is the case or not. First go into a mild trance and look around your house through slightly squinted eyes. If you see any black specks floating, or flitting about in the air, then there is definitely some negativity in the atmosphere – negativity most likely caused by the evil eye.

The best way to get rid of the black specks is to light a stick of Seven African Powers Incense and waft the smoke through and around them. As you do so, say the chant below in a confident voice. Letting out a wild, uncontrolled scream at this point will make absolutely sure that the specks will be banished for good. After you have done this, it is a good idea to sprinkle yourself with holy water, from head to toe, while uttering an incomprehensible chant. Then give your thanks to the powers that have helped you; perhaps leave some fruit or liquor out on a table as an offering.

'In the name of the powerful spirits of Africa,
I bid you black specks of evil to begone!
Never to return!'

Chapter Seven

SHADOW MAGIC

'I'm gonna sprinkle a little goofer dust all round your head,
you'll wake up some of these mornings and
find your own self dead.'

Charles Spand, *Big Fat Mama Blues*, 1930

Voodooists have never fought shy of such dark magical workings as wreaking revenge or cursing enemies. Such actions can be necessary as the world is not always sweetness and light. In Voodoo and Hoodoo, if someone does you or your family harm, there is no question of 'turning the other cheek'. The perpetrator of evil is dealt with in kind. A curse or jinx is laid on them appropriate to the level of evil they have committed. In some cases, the evil doer could be given fair warning that you are about to curse them. This may be enough to deter them from committing further evil against you. But giving fair warning is in no sense compulsory. In fact, it could well give the impression that you are weak and indecisive, and thus easy prey for more wrong doings. In my experience, swift and direct magical justice is usually the best way of dealing with malicious people.

FOOT TRACK MAGIC

Foot Track Magic works on the assumption that a person's footprint can be used as a magical link to affect them in some (usually malevolent) way. For instance, a conjurer might sprinkle Goofer (graveyard) Dust, or Hot Foot Powder (a herb and mineral formula) across a route used by his or her intended victim. Contact between the victim's foot and the powder results in magical 'poisoning', which might take the form of an 'unnatural' illness or a run of bad luck.

To further empower the curse, conjure men and women usually recite an appropriate rhyme or chant, like the one below, as they sprinkle the Goofer Dust

'[name] *when you walk this path,*
Graveyard dirt gonna blight your soul,
No more luck and no more joy,
Hell hound's gonna dog your tail.'

or Hot Foot Powder over their victim's footprint. This is a particularly effective method of dealing with one's enemies. The technique has its roots in the folk beliefs of the Yoruba, Fon and Congo peoples of Africa, and is widely used by Hoodooists.

Foot Track Magic can also be used to make an enemy depart. You simply follow the person until he or she walks on some ground where they will leave a footprint. You then sprinkle Magnetic Sand *(see suppliers, page 125)* into the footprint. Using a shovel, dig up the footprint and place it in a suitable container. You then carry the container to a river or stream, turn your back to the water and throw the contents of the container over your left shoulder into the water. The power of the Magnetic Sand will ensure the person in question will leave town.

Items associated with the feet – socks, shoes, toenails and so on – can also be used to make someone depart. One conjure woman from the southern states of America utilized a novel way of getting rid of a relative who had outstayed his welcome. She took his toenail clippings and pulverized them. She then served them up to him in cornbread. He left shortly afterwards.

There are many voodoo spells for making an enemy or irritating person leave town.

CROSSING AND JINXING

'Crossing' is a variant of Foot Track Magic and involves placing a mark or symbol on a path where the intended victim walks. The mark or symbol is usually drawn in the dust or is laid out with herbs and powders, but crossed needles, pins, nails or brooms are also used. Like in Foot Track Magic, the 'hurt' or curse enters the victim through the feet when he or she walks over the mark. Typical crossing marks include wavy lines, crosses, 'X's and circles. Practitioners often spit upon the marks or crossed items to spiritually activate them.

Another method of cursing someone is to jinx them. This will bring the victim a run of 'unexplained' bad luck, often for years on end. One popular method of jinxing an enemy is to throw a preparation of herbs and powders into their yard or garden. Some appropriate herbs and roots to use for this are: valerian, knot grass, black mustard seed, chicory root and jimson weed. The herbs can be shredded or chopped and the roots powdered in a pestle and mortar. Then the throwing mixture should be placed in a bag or container and the chant at the foot of the page may be recited.

You then go to your victim's house and throw the mixture onto his or her property. For good measure, and assuming no one is in earshot, you might repeat the chant as you do this.

Also popular for jinxing an enemy are candle burning rituals. These are both highly effective and easily performed. First, the altar should be set up with items

'[name] *I curse your luck,*
No good will ever come of you.
From this day forth, all you'll know
Is grief, gloom and misery.'

'Hell, damnation and misery,
Be upon [name],
Nowhere to run, nowhere to hide,
Devil haunt you till you die.'

that will induce an appropriately evil and vengeful mood – burn some Crossing or Damnation Incense, for example. Once everything is set up, anoint a black candle with Jinx Oil, then roll it in powdered knot grass herb. The name of the person you wish to jinx should then be incised on the candle three times – from bottom to top. Place the black candle in a holder and perform a purifying ritual *(see page 19)*. At this point, you light the candle and recite a suitably vengeful verse, along the lines of the one at the top of this page.

Once this is done, perform another purifying ritual and leave the candle to (safely) burn down. Do this ritual at midnight on three consecutive nights.

CHEWING THE ROOT

One of the most terrifying ways of hexing someone is known as 'chewing the root'. This involves the Hoodoo doctor chewing a root (usually Chewing John Root) in the presence of his victim, while making signs and speaking incantations in unknown tongues. The effect of this is understandably terrifying; the doctor swaying from side to side and muttering incomprehensibly, his eyes rolled back, and the juice from the root running down his chin. Usually, the victim is brought to his or her knees, pleading for mercy, in a matter of seconds.

Chewing the root was a speciality of Earl Marlowe. I remember one incident which occurred during the mid-1980s, after our blues–calypso band had played a successful date at a London venue. Quite a crowd had attended the gig and we looked forward to going home with a sizeable wad of cash. Unfortunately, the organizer of the event had other ideas and, after giving us a lame excuse, absconded without giving us our agreed cut of the door money. Rather down-hearted, we all packed up our gear and left.

But Earl was not going to take the promoter's dishonourable behaviour lying down. The following day, he called me, telling me that 'We gotta job to do,' and that I should meet him in a north London bar. When I arrived, Earl informed me that, through his contacts, he had the promoter's home address and that we were shortly going to convince him of the error of his ways. I was a little apprehensive as I knew the promoter had some heavy contacts, not averse to carrying firearms on occasion. I raised this point with Earl.

'Power of the root will burn him over,' he replied.

Once we had finished our drinks, we made our way to the large town house where the promoter lived. Earl confidently banged the door three times. After a couple of minutes, the promoter appeared. He didn't look pleased to see us.

'We've come for what we're owed,' Earl told him, putting on his sunglasses, through which he glared menacingly at the promoter.

The promoter was not impressed and a look of sheer malice overtook his face. 'You two,' he said very slowly, his voice clearly quivering with rage, 'had better get on your bikes a bit sharpish, otherwise I will be forced to personally *rip your heads off*!'

Being decapitated was not the kind of end I would have chosen for myself – given the choice, that is. So I quietly

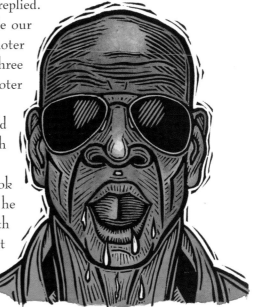

Earl Marlowe puts a hex on a greedy music promoter by 'chewing the root'.

suggested to Earl that we leave. Earl, apparently unperturbed by the violent outburst, ignored me and continued to stare at the promoter. Then he pulled a small, gnarled-looking root out of his pocket, put it in his mouth and began to methodically chew on it. A moment or so later, he started to grunt and mutter incomprehensibly, and then began pacing up and down, his body shaking all over.

'What's he doing?' the promoter asked nervously – by this time, Earl's 'unknown tongues' had taken on a distinctly inhuman quality. Then, despite his age, Earl leapt up the steps and let out a falsetto shriek right in the face of the promoter. The effect was electrifying. A look of horror overtook the promoter's face and then he passed out cold.

The very next day we were paid in full. The promoter even put in a bonus.

SUFFERING ROOT

Not all hexes, however, are justified. In his book *Blue Roots*, American writer Roger Pinckney relates how a number of years ago a white attorney from South Carolina hired a Gullah (black) housekeeper, but later dismissed her because he found her surly and unmotivated. The woman left the house in a huff, muttering about rooting or hexing her former employer.

A new housekeeper was hired, and, on her first day on the job, she discovered three brand-new sewing needles tied together with black thread and stuck beneath the couple's mattress. The maid recognized it as a Suffering Root. She showed the 'root' to her employers and then threw the needles into the stove, urging the attorney's wife to seek immediate help from a Hoodoo doctor. The wife laughed the incident off – until the following morning when she awoke to find her skin covered with a scaly rash. She then sought help, not from a conjure man, but from a medical specialist in Charleston. The diagnosis: a severe bout of chicken pox, the worst the doctor had ever seen. A day later, her infant son also came down with the pox.

A month later, they had both recovered, but then the attorney himself was stricken with severe abdominal pain. He was rushed to hospital for an emergency appendectomy. As it happened, an older son was already there for a long-scheduled removal of his tonsils. But during the operation something went wrong. The boy stopped breathing and was revived only after much effort by the panicked doctors.

Both father and son eventually went home, but their troubles were far from over.

The attorney suffered a long series of debilitating post-operative infections. Then, on a visit to his physician, he was struck by the similarity between the stitches holding together his infected incision and the needles tied with black thread found beneath his mattress. He immediately demanded the stitches be removed. The doctor protested. It was too early, especially considering infection had delayed the healing process. But the attorney persisted and the doctor complied. Two days later, he was completely healed. Neither he nor any member of his family suffered any further inexplicable and catastrophic ailments.

STRESS-RELATED DEATHS?

Stories like these make it clear that you're a fool if you don't respect the power of the root or hex. Apart from anything else, there is documented evidence that people can and do die from curses and hexes. Behavioural science explains away such deaths as resulting from shock, due to prolonged and intense emotion – namely, fear. On the surface, this seems to be a perfectly reasonable argument, especially considering the level of fear some Hoodoo doctors inspire in their local communities. However, statistics reveal that there is an almost total absence of stress-related death in other extremely stressful situations – such as during earthquakes, tornadoes or hurricanes. Indeed, even hostages who are under daily threat of death, do not die from stress. It seems that humans can tolerate an incredible degree of stress – so long as there is no root or hex involved.

WARNING AN ENEMY OFF

If someone is causing you a degree of grief and you want to warn them off, then the following Voodoo doll spell should do the trick. Set up your altar and light two black candles, dressed with Go Away Oil. Get Away Incense could also be burned. Now place the doll on your altar and slowly push three pins into its head. As you do so, recite the chant at the foot of the page.

Now put the doll in a sealed container and bury it in the ground. After three days, unearth the doll and take it to your enemy. Show it to them and explain that they have got a choice: they either stop causing you grief and you will remove the curse (by ritually removing the pins from the doll), or else they opt to continue causing you grief, in which case you will leave the curse intact, and their pains will get worse and worse.

When confronted in this way, most troublesome people are reduced to jibbering skunk dogs, begging for mercy.

'Pins of pain bring [name] *an ache in the head,*
make him/her regret all they've done and said.'

⬩ DR ALEXANDER'S DEATH CURSE ⬩

This is a highly potent curse, formulated by Dr Alexander, a nineteenth-century New Orleans Voodoo priest. But it is offered here for *curiosity value only*, and you are strongly advised *not* to use it. Not only is there more than enough malice in the world, but curses have a habit of rebounding – unless you are a very experienced sorcerer, in which case you would have little need to curse anyone.

This is best performed at midnight on a full moon. First write your enemy's name on parchment in Dove's Blood Ink and place it in an incense burner. Then add the following.

1 teaspoon of rosemary
4 teaspoons of frankincense
6 teaspoons of lavender incense
2 teaspoons of myrrh incense
4 teaspoons of orris powder
1 teaspoon of patchouli leaves
½ teaspoon of saltpetre
6 teaspoons of sandalwood incense
1 teaspoon of cinnamon

Now use Dragon's Blood Incense to draw a circle around your burner, and lay a piece of lodestone in front of it. Add the Dragon's Blood Incense to the burner and light it. As the mixture burns, visualize how your enemy could meet their demise. Then go to bed leaving the mixture to smoulder.

'Do this for seven nights,' advised Dr Alexander, 'and your enemy will be destroyed.' To further empower the hex, the good Doctor suggested placing a little of the mixture in a red mojo bag and throwing it on to your enemy's property.

DANGERS OF CURSING

Cursing, even if the intent is less severe than Dr Alexander's Black Curse, can rebound on the perpetrator in tragic ways, as the following story shows.

In 1938, in a parish not far from New Orleans, the Reverend Howard Randle cut his wife's throat because he believed she had put a spell on him. His wife, Lucinda, had been jealous of the female members of her husband's congregation, especially those he visited regularly. In a moment of pique, she called on a Voodoo doctor and purchased some powder to put in her husband's coffee; the powder, said the doctor, had the power to render impotent any man who consumed it. Randle drank the coffee, and almost immediately Lucinda lost her nerve.

Overcome with remorse, and fearing that the powder might have even more drastic effects than the Voodoo doctor predicted, she began to scream, 'I've killed you! I've killed you!' and proceeded to tell Randle what she had done. After convincing him he was about to die, she fell to her knees and begged him to kill her.

To discuss the issue, the couple went walking in the woods together. Lucinda again implored Randle to kill her. She told him she never wanted to be separated from him, and that because the 'fix' had doomed him to die, the only way they could remain together was if she died too.

'I figured I was gonna die anyway,' Randle told police later, 'and I didn't want Lucinda left alone. She said she wanted to go first and that she'd be waiting for me by the river in that glorious land where we would live forever. I took out my knife and she closed her eyes. Then I cut her throat. It didn't hurt her at all. She just raised one leg, let it drop, and she was dead.'

Lucinda had to wait a long time by the river – Randle received a life sentence for her murder.

➤ HIGH-LEVEL HEXING ➤

Hexing is more prevalent than most people imagine. Although not widely reported, it is known to have been utilized by various military dictators. For example, when US forces invaded Panama in 1989, resulting in the imprisonment of General Noriega, they found some unusual items in his mansion. These included a large table covered with glass-cased candles, strange-looking statues and little cloth bags containing various powders, which were assumed to be drugs. When analysed, however, the powders were found to be a mixture of herbs and incenses. Later it was discovered that General Noriega had in his employ one or more sorcerers of Brazilian, Cuban or Puerto Rican extraction, whom it was said had been performing hexes against the Americans on behalf of the General.

The late Idi Amin of Uganda was also known to have extensively employed black magicians, working in the African sorcery tradition. One account claims that Amin abducted someone who had offended him, and that one of the most powerful sorcerers for hire in Africa slowly skinned the abductee alive in a ritual to capture his soul, in order to make it a slave for Idi Amin. More recently, many Santeria and Voodoo practitioners have speculated that the mysterious and elusive 'Gulf War Syndrome' was the result of a massive hexing performed by Saddam Hussein.

Chapter Eight

SOOTHSAYING

'Well I'm going to Newport to see Aunt Caroline Dye,
She's a fortune teller, oh Lord, she sure don't tell no lie.'

Johnny Temple, *Hoodoo Woman*, 1937

'Tarot cards are just fancy shit,' rasped Earl, as we sat under a big oak on Hampstead Heath, the green lungs of north London. 'You don't need 'em to get a take on the future. Way I see it, a deck a playing cards'll do just as well, if not better.' He was running through the rudiments of fortune telling with playing cards. A dog-eared deck of cards was spread out, face down, on a purple satin cloth on the grass.

'Pull a card,' he instructed, 'and keep it face down.'

I held the flat of my hand over the cards for a moment, then selected one that seemed to stand out. I laid it on the cloth, away from the other cards. Earl picked it up and for some reason scrutinized the Chinese dragon design on the back. After a second or so, he said, 'I see some very unusual currents of energy circulating in luminous globules around your etheric body. This configuration of crystalline droplets makes me 100 per cent certain that the spirits have picked you out to learn the secrets of the Rattler, the desert dreamer.'

'The what?' I asked, completely mystified.

'The Rattler,' he repeated. 'But I can say no more on this until after the dark of the moon.'

'Oh, come on!' I protested. 'You can't set me up like that, without explaining what you mean.'

He shook his head. 'The less said, the better. You'll meet the Rattler soon enough.'

As he was unwilling to elaborate further, I decided to risk pointing out what seemed to me to be a fatal flaw in his card-reading technique.

'Don't you turn the cards face up when you read them?'

'Never needed to; only confuses the issue,' he replied, looking very nettled that I should dare to point this out. He then explained that any conjure worker, or soothsayer, worth their salt, never turns the cards the right way up during a reading. 'The backs are where the real auguries are encoded,' he insisted. He did, however, concede that it might be necessary, certainly at first, to learn the conventional techniques of card reading in order to progress to the more 'advanced technique' of reading the backs. 'Apart from anything else,' continued Earl, 'most people expect you to read the fronts. But the fact is, reading the fronts ain't nowhere near as powerful as reading the reverse sides.'

The 'back' or 'front' issue aside, Earl was a great believer in the accuracy of playing cards when it came to divining the future. He saw them as particularly valuable when it came to putting someone on the right course in life.

'Lotta people tend to drift through life. They got no idea where they goin', nor where they come from. They got no notion of their destiny. But show them their destiny and bang! Everything fits into place. They got a purpose in life. Just like the planets that circle the sun, they found their orbit. They got no doubt; they flow with the power of the cosmos. Discover your destiny and your life will be fulfilled.'

FANNY MOSEBURY

So far as Earl was concerned, a good card reader can reveal a person's destiny – and therefore change a person's life. 'Friend o' mine, Fanny Mosebury, who lived down in New Orleans during the 1930s, turned a man's life around with a card reading,' said Earl. 'She was one scary psychic, believe me. Spirits hung out in her house all the time. They'd appear in her bedroom and turn her mattress upside down or else they'd take the feathers out of it and leave 'em strewn across the floor. One time a spirit even stomped on her roof, blocked her chimney and caused her front room to fill up with smoke.'

Earl lay back against the oak tree, his legs stretched out, and proceeded to tell me the following story.

One night, there was a man sitting on Fanny's doorstep. She knew him slightly and knew that his name was Howard, and that he had left his wife when she had become pregnant to take up with another woman. Not that this particularly bothered Fanny; people's business is their own, was her attitude. But Fanny knew that one of the spirits in her house – Marie Laveau – didn't like Howard; so, for his own good, she told him to move away from her property – otherwise that spirit might cause him trouble.

But Howard scorned her warning, saying, 'I ain't scared of no spirit doing nothin' to me, ha! ha!' He then defiantly lit a cigar, and began to puff clouds of smoke into Fanny's face. Having done all she could to warn him, she closed the door on him.

Suddenly a chill came over Howard, and his cigar went out. His hands began to tremble, and when he attempted to get up to run away he found himself frozen to the spot. Then something that felt like a heavy hand pushed his hat over his eyes and slapped him across the face. When he attempted to call Fanny, the invisible hand pressed his mouth closed, and a voice said, 'Go and pray and respect.'

Eventually, he was able to move again and lifted his hat from his eyes. As he did so, he saw a very beautiful girl of mixed race standing near to him – it was Marie Laveau. Then she vanished as suddenly as she appeared.

In a panic, Howard flew up the steps to Fanny's house and banged frantically on her door. Fanny took him into her house, which was a gloomy place with pictures of saints pinned to the walls, red lamps burning and Catholic images on every table and dresser. When he related what had happened, she gave him a crucifix to wear and told him to go back to his wife and never to leave her.

Marie Laveau,
Voodoo Queen of New Orleans.

'No way,' he said. 'My wife threatened me with a knife and I don't want to see her again.'

Fanny pulled out a deck of cards from the drawer of her dresser and cut it four times. 'I see a fight,' she said, 'and it was the night you beat her. I see blood and a torn dress, and I see a child crying, and a pistol on a table right by a Bible. But I don't see no knife.'

'She had it hidden in her dress,' said Howard, 'she sho' had.'

Fanny cut the deck again and spread the cards out on the table. 'Cards show that she ain't had a knife, but told you she had, and she'd cut your hand if you reached for the gun. You had already hit her and made her nose bleed.'

She had described the fight exactly as it had occurred. Howard began to tremble again. 'How'd those cards tell you all that? Lord have mercy; that's just how it was. I feel something comin' on me. I can't stop trembling. Oh, Lord, Miss Fanny, give me a drink of whiskey, please!'

Being of a pious disposition, Fanny had no whiskey, but gave him a dose of aromatic spirits of ammonia, which she kept for her own frequent use (she was in a constant state of shock due to the antics of the spirits that haunted her house).

Howard soon revived and the trembling stopped. 'I see no other way,' he said. 'And I'm going … I'm going back to Martha, Lord help me.'

THE PREACHER MAN

Howard was true to his word and went back to his wife. And soon afterwards, his whole life was changed around. After studying theology and philosophy, he became a charismatic preacher of no mean ability. His services pulled a big congregation due to the quality of the singing and music. Central to Howard's services were the 'sisters', who were all supposed to be blessed with psychic powers and at intervals wandered through the congregation offering to pray for those who were sick or had troubles of one sort or another.

MEANINGS OF THE CARDS

'That's how a man discovered his destiny through a card reading,' Earl concluded. At that point, we adjourned to the café on the far northern fringes of the heath. As we sipped our tea, Earl instructed me in the basics of conventional playing-card reading. This was something he was loath to do, as he wholeheartedly believed in abstract methods of conjure, epitomized by reading the backs, rather than the fronts of cards. But he relented on the premise that 'clients'll think you're crazy if you don't adhere to some conventional structures.'

I frantically took notes as Earl reeled off a list of meanings for the four suits of the average 52-card deck of playing cards. You may like to use these meanings for your own experiments with the art of divining the future. They are listed here more or less as Earl related them that summer's day.

DIAMONDS

ACE: Money and wealth.

KING: A fair-featured man with a violent temper and a vindictive, obstinate turn of mind.

QUEEN: A fair-featured woman, flirtatious and fond of parties and admiration.

JACK: A near relative who puts his own interests first, is self-opinionated and easily offended.

TEN: Plenty of money. Possibly a marriage with several children.

NINE: If next to positive cards, it implies a pleasant surprise connected with money; but next to negative cards, it signifies 'crossed swords'.

EIGHT: A permanent relationship late in life which will likely be somewhat chequered.

SEVEN: Be careful – hard times and money problems may lie ahead. Beware uncharitable tongues.

SIX: The end of a serious relationship. Be very careful about rushing into another one.

FIVE: Unexpected news, or success in business enterprises.

FOUR: A confidence is betrayed.

THREE: Legal and domestic quarrels. Unhappiness caused by a partner's irritability.

DEUCE: A tempestuous love affair which causes opposition from relatives or friends.

SPADES

ACE: Trouble, danger, even an augury of death.

KING: An ambitious and successful, dark-featured man who could be dangerous.

QUEEN: A malicious and unscrupulous woman, fond of scandal and open to bribes.

JACK: A well-meaning but lazy person.

TEN: An evil omen. Possibly grief or incarceration. This card has power to undermine good cards near to it.

NINE: An ill-fated card foretelling sickness, loss and family feuds.

EIGHT: A warning regarding any current enterprises. Possibly evil and opposition from friends.

SEVEN: Sorrow caused by the loss of a dear friend.

SIX: After an intense period of hard work, comes both rest and wealth.

FIVE: Another's bad temper may interfere with your life; but happiness can be found with the one you love.

FOUR: Pay great attention to business and finances.

THREE: A relationship that will be marred by infidelity – either on your or your partner's part. A possible journey.

DEUCE: Moving home.

CLUBS

ACE: General prosperity. A peaceful home life.

KING: A dark-featured, high-minded man, who makes a reliable friend and a faithful lover.

QUEEN: A trusting and affectionate, dark-featured woman, who is attractive to men, but not taken in by flattery.

JACK: A loyal and generous friend.

TEN: Sudden riches, possibly from a legacy or a lottery win.

NINE: Discord resulting from the opposition of friends or relatives.

EIGHT: A passion for financial speculation or gambling.

SEVEN: Great happiness and good fortune, but if trouble is encountered it will be caused by someone of the opposite sex.

SIX: Success in business.

FIVE: An advantageous relationship or marriage.

FOUR: Beware deceit and double-dealing.

THREE: Marrying into money.

DEUCE: Disappointment and opposition.

HEARTS

ACE: An important card. On its own, it represents the home. If next to hearts, it implies love, friendship and affection; next to diamonds, money or news of distant friends; beside spades, it foretells disagreements, misunderstandings, contention or misfortune; by clubs, and you will have to work to get what you want.

KING: A good-hearted man with strong emotions, but given to rash judgements and possessing more zeal than discretion.

QUEEN: A fair-featured woman, loving and loveable, prudent and faithful.

JACK: Neither male or female, sometimes it is taken to represent Cupid or the best friend of the inquirer. The cards on either side indicate the good or bad nature of its intentions.

TEN: Good fortune. Happiness and the possibility of a large family. This card negates the influence of any bad cards in a reading and confirms good ones.

NINE: Wishes fulfilled. The degree to which they are fulfilled depends on the surrounding cards.

EIGHT: An enjoyable and busy social life.

SEVEN: An unreliable, possibly untrustworthy friend, who may prove to be an enemy.

SIX: Your naturally trusting nature could be easy prey for con artists.

FIVE: Groundless jealousy.

FOUR: Danger of being 'left on the shelf' due to being over critical and hard to please in relationships.

THREE: Tact and discretion are called for.

DEUCE: Prosperity and success – the degree of which depends on the surrounding cards.

THE JOKER

I always include a Joker in my deck for fortune telling. If you decide to do the same, then the Joker should be viewed as the wild card. It signifies raw power and untameable force. If it comes up when you do a reading, you can be sure that something unpredictable and awe-inspiring is about to pass through your life (or through the life of your inquirer). Whether this is of a positive nature or not depends on the cards surrounding the Joker. But even this is not a reliable indicator with the wild card: all you can really do is wait and see what occurs. When the Joker is around, events are in the hands of fate.

THE FOUR-CARD SPREAD

Once you have memorized the meanings of the cards, you need to sort out a spread for organizing your readings. Earl taught me a simple one, called the four-card spread, which can be used on a daily basis to see how things are going in your life generally. It shows the circumstances surrounding the present, the recent past and the near future. By far the best way to begin any divinatory reading is to first get yourself into a mild trance state, then perform a cleansing ritual (but don't worry about taking too long over this; the main thing is to sprinkle some holy water around the area you are doing the reading in). Next give the cards a thorough shuffle and cut the deck three times.

THE FOUR-CARD SPREAD

(1) *What is going on in your life at present*
(2) *The biggest influence in your life at present*
(3) *The recent past*
(4) *The near future*

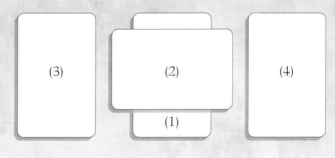

You then pull four cards from the deck and lay them out, face up, as shown above. The first card should be placed vertically on the table in front of you; the second placed horizontally over the first, forming a cross; the third put on the left side of the crossed cards; and the fourth on the right side of the crossed cards.

The first card represents what is going on in your life now. The second card shows the biggest influence in your life at present. The third card reveals the recent past, the fourth the near future.

This is an ideal spread for beginners, as it is simple to perform and is also surprisingly accurate. Personally, however, I usually work in a more free-form manner. If I'm doing a reading for a client, I first find out what is on their mind, partly by talking to them, but also by observing their body language, and so on. Then I shuffle the cards, and lay out the whole deck one by one, reading the meanings as I go. I don't always go through the complete deck – my intuition sometimes tells me it is time to stop, as we've got all the information we need. I also use this method when I am doing readings for myself – although, to save time, I often draw out nine cards, rather than going through the lot. It all depends on the importance of the reading.

Readings done first thing in the morning to ascertain conditions surrounding the day ahead work well using nine cards. Interpret the first three as referring to the morning, the second three to the afternoon, the third three to the evening.

◂ CARD CONJURE ▸

You can use playing cards to good effect in spells and conjure. Instead of divining the future with them, you set about changing it. First, select the cards you would ideally like to see come up in a divination reading. For instance, if you wished to attain success in business, you might choose the following cards: six of clubs, ace of diamonds, deuce of hearts and the nine of hearts. Once you have selected the appropriate cards, perform a cleansing ritual and burn the appropriate incense (such as Success Incense for success in business). Then, using a Voodoo or lucky mojo doll, you perform a mock divination ritual, with the doll taking the role of a powerful psychic reader. You place your selected cards in front of the fortune teller, as if he or she were reading your fortune. Make it as 'real' as possible. Mimic his or her voice out loud – gasp at how fortuitous the reading is and say something like, 'I see in the cards that you are going to be very, very rich. A business venture is going to exceed your wildest expectations ....' Repeat this kind of dialogue until it becomes a chant. Once you feel the spell has met its mark, perform a closing ritual and wrap the doll, along with the cards, in a white cloth and bury them in some 'holy ground', so the 'seeds' of success (or whatever the intent of your spell) can germinate and grow. (Use your intuition to find your holy ground – it may be an ancient sacred site, or it could be in your own back yard.)

THE WORLD BEHIND THE MIRROR

When we'd finished our tea, Earl and I decided to take a final stroll across the heath before heading home. I took the opportunity to question him further about the reading he had done for me earlier.

He stopped for a moment then, almost in a whisper, said, 'The reading showed me that it will soon be time for you and me to travel in our spirit bodies to the world behind the mirror.'

Great, I thought, I ask for elucidation and he gets even more cryptic. 'And how do we go about that?' I asked with growing impatience.

He grinned somewhat mischievously. 'We eat some sacred fungi, then we meet the guardian of the crossroads and ask his permission to enter the spirit realm. Better hang on to your hat, though, 'cause things can turn seriously hairy there.'

I gulped, not relishing the prospect of this at all. 'In what way?' I enquired.

'Well, for one thing, you're destined to meet the Rattler, the desert dreamer,' he answered, still grinning and obviously relishing my trepidation. 'My vision tells me he is your ally or power animal. He's a tricky one – very powerful – but tricky. He'll either accept you or he won't. If he doesn't accept you, then watch out! He'll swallow you whole – soul and all.'

BRER RABBIT AND THE BONE TRICK

After I'd left Earl and was on my way home, I mused on the outlandish, upside-down card reading Earl had done for me – and on the even more outlandish interpretation.

'How can you read the backs of cards, when they are all exactly the same?' I asked myself. And who, or what, was the desert dreamer, the eater of souls?

The whole thing reminded me of a tale about Brer Rabbit I'd been read as a boy. One time old Brer Rabbit was thinking up ways he could outwit Brer Bear and get his hands on the vegetables he was growing on his patch. Brer Rabbit had been too busy lazing around in the spring sunshine to have grown any provisions himself that year and so thought he'd take advantage of someone else's hard work.

He went up to Brer Bear and said to him, 'Brer Bear, I sees you grown a fine vegetable patch, this year. Now I wouldn't want any harm to come to it, no sir. But I been casting them bones the old soothsayer give me, and they says that a whole sack full of your potatoes's gonna git dug up by a thief, this very night.'

'Why, thanks for warning me, Brer Rabbit, you is a true friend,' said Brer Bear.

That night Brer Bear heeded Brer Rabbit's warning and sat up with a big stick guarding his vegetable patch. Wily old Brer Rabbit sat in a nearby bush, biding his time. When he heard Brer Bear begin to snore, he took his chance and dug up a sackful of potatoes and ran off home with them.

The following day, Brer Bear went up to Brer Rabbit and said, 'Brer Rabbit, you was right about a thief digging up my potatoes in the night and running off with them. I sat up guarding them. Only problem was I fell asleep and the thief got away with them. Now, what with you being wise an' all, specially when it come to fortune tellin', I'm thinking that maybe if you guarded my vegetable patch, the thief wouldn't catch you nappin'. If you do me this favour, I'll give you a generous share o' my vegetables.'

Brer Rabbit agreed to guard Brer Bear's vegetable plot for a share of the vegetables. But, of course, as he himself was the only vegetable thief in the neighbourhood, he didn't exactly have to be a vigilant guard. In fact, he slept soundly all night.

The following morning Brer Bear was overjoyed to find that no one had stolen his vegetables and congratulated Brer Rabbit on having done a fine job of guarding the vegetable patch. As a reward, he gave Brer Rabbit a whole sack full of vegetables to take home and promised him more if he continued to guard his vegetable patch.

Brer Rabbit was the Afro-American slave version of the trickster of African folklore. He was always up to mischief. But sometimes his mischief-making got out of hand. And I was beginning to think that this is what had happened with Earl. Could I trust him? I was starting to wonder ....

⌐ ORACLES OF SANTERIA ⌐

High priests of Santeria, known as 'babalaos', generally use two systems of divination: the Ifá and the Caracoles. The oracle of Ifá consists of a body of sacred stories (patakíes) that a babalao memorizes. By casting a small chain with eight concave, oval or round pieces of leather, coconut or calabash rind attached to it, the babalao obtains a configuration that indicates which 'oddu', or chapter, of the oracle of Ifá is to be recited at a particular moment for a particular inquirer. These stories are usually very ambiguous; the babalao must rely on his magically inspired intuition to find the correct application of the story to the situation.

Although considered highly reliable, the Ifá oracle is not sought as often as the Caracoles, or cowrie shells, which are said to be the mouths of the orishas (gods). The Caracoles is much simpler than the Ifá system. While as many as 256 oddus appear in Ifá, only 16 'letras' (equivalent of oddus) are evident in Caracoles divination. Sixteen cowrie shells are cast; the number of shells that fall with the natural opening facing up determines with letra is to be recited.

Chapter Nine

VOODOO SPIRITS

*'Three days my body must lie silent and
fasting while my spirit went wherever spirits must go
that seek answers never given to men as men.'*

Zora Neale Hurston, *Mules and Men*, 1935

'It will soon be time to embark on our journey,' announced Earl, his dark eyes dancing in the candlelit room. 'The Rattler – the desert dreamer – is eager to meet you.' A shiver went through me as he said this. I really did not want to go on some enigmatic journey to meet spirits and power animals. Apart from any other considerations, I'd been having bad dreams about a huge rattle-snake coiling itself round me, its cold eyes staring into mine, and its tongue flitting out; and all the time, its tail rattling the heavy staccato of the bongo drums. In fact, at that point, I'd come to the conclusion that I couldn't trust Earl. He was unpredictable and I just didn't know what he would do next.

VOODOO ODYSSEY

That winter's evening, however, Earl had invited me round to his place. He'd prepared a delicious meal of spicy beef stew with mushrooms and peppers. It was clearly a reconciliatory gesture on Earl's part, knowing that I had grown apprehensive about the direction in which his teachings had progressed. Once we'd finished our meal, we sat down in his tatty armchairs to drink bourbon. This helped me to relax. In fact, while Earl related various tales from the Caribbean, I relaxed to the point that I fell into a dreamy reverie. Staring at the bottle, I noticed that the flickering candlelight reflected in the glass seemed to be jumping on to the tabletop, where it transformed into tiny fairy-like people who danced with wild abandon. I squeezed my eyes shut, then opened them again, but the 'fairies' continued to dance.

Suddenly, a terrible panic overwhelmed me. I leapt to my feet and pointed a finger at Earl. 'You spiked the food with magic mushrooms, didn't you?!'

'Well, I told you, it's time for our journey,' he replied.

'You should've asked me first. It's incredibly irresponsible,' I ranted, in a fury.

At this he burst out laughing, slapping his thigh in his mirth. 'You're too much,' he spluttered. 'You say you want to learn the secrets of Hoodoo, and then you chicken out when the serious business begins. You can't have it two ways, man; if you can't take the heat, then get out of the kitchen.'

'Well, you haven't exactly given me much choice,' I complained.

He then got up and put his hand on my shoulder and, with a kindly look, said, 'I wouldn't be doing this if the spirits hadn't marked you out. Don't worry, I'm with you 100 per cent of the way. Every novice of the spirit world has to have his guide – and I'm yours.'

'But what happens next?' I asked, calming down a little.

He shrugged and said, 'Can't predict what the spirits are gonna do. We have to wait and see. Ride it out.'

A MAN OF WEALTH AND FAME

Just at that moment came three sharp knocks on Earl's door. I nearly jumped out of my skin, but Earl didn't flinch. With a knowing nod, he got up and answered the door. When he came back into the room, he said, 'Journey's 'bout to begin.' I looked up and behind Earl was the visitor. It was an Afro-Latino-looking man, dressed in a black leather chauffeur's uniform, complete with cap and shades.

He held out his hand to me, 'Pleased to meet you,' he said. Then, with a wide grin, added, 'I think you probably guessed my name.'

'Yeah, he's a man of wealth and fame,' put in Earl.

My blood ran cold.

'Truth is, I'm a man o' many names. But you can call me Papa Legba,' said the chauffeur, with a smile.

'I'm the dark man, the weaver of the web. I drive the car and open the gates.' He then sat down in an armchair and

poured himself a large bourbon. Slugging it back, he said, 'Ahhh, nectar to an old devil's taste buds.' He put the glass down, then added, 'Car's waitin' outside. Grab ya coats boys. Time to hit the road.'

Even though, by then, events had turned decidedly weird, I decided to follow them through. So I picked up my coat and followed Earl and Legba down the stairs. Outside was a black Daimler. As we walked up to the vehicle, I noticed that a large black spider was spinning its web on the chrome bonnet ornament. Legba held the back door open for Earl and I. We climbed in; Legba shut the door and got into the driver's seat. He checked the mirror, then gunned the powerful engine. 'Yee Hah!' he yelled. 'Let's get outta this town!'

We drove off through the city streets. As we crossed the river, the landscape outside began to blur and London landmarks simply faded out, as we entered a grey, all-encompassing mist. Earl lit a cigarette; the flash of the match momentarily illuminated the gloom. 'It's the mist of limbo,' he informed me. Soon I started to see forms in the mist, strange swirling shapes, and voices ....

INTO THE ABSTRACT REALM

When the mist and visions abated, we found ourselves driving down a dirt track, lined by tall cypress trees. Eventually we arrived at a large farm gate, which was wide open. We drove through and were suddenly confronted with what looked like a rock festival. A sea of people and tents stretched out into the distance. Music played and I could make out a stage, with towering PA speakers, some distance away.

Papa Legba drew the car to a halt, jumped out and held the back door open for us to get out. 'Come on, boys, time for me to leave you.' Referring to me, he added, 'Kid here's got an appointment with the Crawlin' King Snake.'

We climbed out, said goodbye to Legba, then watched him drive off along the route we came in on. We then walked deep into the heart of the crowd. Thousands of people, of all nationalities, dressed in wild and colourful clothes were at the festival. Some were selling clothes, others food and drink. But the majority were down by the stage areas, listening to the bands.

'This is unreal,' I said to Earl.

A serious expression came on to his face. 'One day,' he said, 'you will come to know that this is more real than the everyday reality you're familiar with. Keep your eyes open for anything unusual. It might only be a momentary thing, a glimpse, but the moment you see it you will know. And you must follow it immediately – do you understand? Don't wait for me, just go straight after it.'

'But everything is unusual here. How am I supposed to tell the difference?' When I turned round, he was gone.

'Earl!' I yelled, dashing through the crowd and around the tents. But there was no sign of him. Then the sea of tents and people, the very festival itself, seemed to fade into the background. It was still discernible, but everything went quiet and took on a dreamlike hue. Up ahead, and clearly tangible, was a tent, much like a fortune-teller's tent, covered in intricate symbols. I decided this was the sign Earl insisted I look out for. So I tentatively entered the tent.

To my astonishment, a life-size rabbit sat behind a table with a crystal ball on it. It grinned and said, 'Wowee! Another customer. Business sure is brisk today. Like your fortune told? Or'd you like to purchase my elixir of life? It's one hell of a remedy; guaranteed to make ya live to 150. Serious medica-tion made outa bourbon, gunpowder and cocaine …. But no, I sees you is a special visitor. You an upside-down man come to see the Rattler, the desert dreamer. Wait here one moment, an' I'll go an' fetch him.'

POWERFUL INDIAN

The rabbit left via the back of the tent and I heard him calling for someone. Moments later an old man came in. He looked like an archetypal Native American shaman: long grey hair, feathered head-dress and bones hanging on a cord around his neck. I recognized him as the 'Powerful Indian' spirit of Hoodoo lore. He sat cross-legged on a cushion on the floor and motioned me to follow suit.

'Like Rabbit said, you're an upside-down man,' he declared in a slow, deep voice. 'Upside-down man is a sorcerer. Everything he does is contrary, upside down, to the average person. He walks between the worlds and talks with the spirits. Doesn't mean you any more special than anyone else who walks this beautiful earth; just means the spirits marked you out to do a job o' work – a job o' helpin' people.' He went quiet for a moment and in that silence I knew utter peace and utter joy. Then he looked me straight in the eyes and said, 'Follow the path o' good. Turn your back on the bad. Look to the rainbow and follow the flight of the eagle. You an earth sorcerer, but it don't hurt to look up at the sky once in a while.' With that, he got up, walked over to me and laid the palms of his hands on my head. 'They call me the Rattler, the desert dreamer. I'm the Crawlin' King Snake all those blues songs spoke of; and you 'bout to become the Snakeman. You gonna crawl the earth and sing your song. Sing it well …. Sing it well ….' At that moment his whole body began to coalesce into a shimmering light, which then flew down to the floor and turned into a snake – a rattlesnake – which slithered across the floor and out of the back of the tent.

THE FERRYMAN

I left the tent to go in search of Earl. The festival had now disappeared completely. In its place was a swirling mist, very much like the mist of limbo we'd encountered previously. I called Earl's name a few times, but got no reply. So I walked and walked, seemingly getting nowhere. After a while, though, I heard the sound of lapping water and eventually came across a river. Due to the mist, I couldn't see the other side, but somehow I felt it was very wide. Suddenly, as I was staring out into the mist, a voice came from downriver.

'Hey, it's the Snakeman!' I recognized the voice as Papa Legba's and, through the mist, could just make out his face. I walked closer and saw that he was on a ferryboat, holding a pole. Beside him was Earl.

'Earl!' I exclaimed, 'I've been looking everywhere for you.'

He sat quietly for a moment, as if musing on my statement, then said, 'You shoulda looked nowhere for me, then you'd a found me.'

'We've got to find a way back home,' I said, not wishing at that point to get caught up in abstract metaphysics.

'I'm not comin' home,' he said quietly. 'It's time for me to sail down the River of Destiny. Papa Legba's takin' me.'

'No,' I said, desperately. 'We've got to get back.'

Earl shook his head. I reached out my hand to him, but before I could reach him, Papa Legba began heaving the ferryboat out into the water.

'Goodbye,' called Earl. 'Don't shed no tears. You the Snakeman now, the Snakeman ... Snakeman ... Snakeman ....'

As Earl's voice faded in the mist, the strange otherworld I was in seemed to fade out too. For a moment that reached into eternity, I found myself in a strange state of non-being. I had no thoughts. I could neither see, hear, feel, taste or smell anything. Yet in some form, I continued to exist. All worldly, material aspects of my being had been stripped away and I was experiencing my deepest self. I was one with my soul or spirit. At some point in this timeless, spaceless state, my senses slowly reactivated and I found myself lying on some damp grass. Rolling over, I recognized that I was on Hampstead Heath. I had no idea how I got there. Whatever had happened the previous night had left me utterly disorientated and confused. Little did I know that worse was to come.

LAST RITES

Rather than go home, I decided to find Earl to see if he could shed any light on the night's events. When I got to his place, no one was around, so I went along to the domino club to see if anyone there knew where he was. A couple of his friends took me aside and, with solemn faces, told me that Earl had been rushed to hospital during the night with some kind of sudden illness and had died in the early hours of the morning. I was stunned and fell into a state of shock. What with Earl's death and the events of the previous night, my set notions about reality had been completely overturned. I had to accept something which defied all rationality – the possibility that, the night before in the spiritworld, I had seen Earl depart for the realm of the dead, ferried by Papa Legba. However, the story wasn't yet over.

INFINITY

Just before Earl's funeral, something prompted me to check his body. I found the coffin hadn't yet been screwed down, so I looked inside and, to my horror, the body inside the coffin wasn't Earl's. I shut my eyes, then opened them again. I wasn't seeing things; it definitely was not Earl. After the service, I mentioned this to a couple of Earl's closest friends, but they said I was seeing things and that I should forget it. Maybe I was hallucinating, I thought. Deep down, however, I now know what I saw. Various indicators over subsequent years have led me to believe that, when Earl sailed down the River of Destiny with Papa Legba, he bodily left this earth for infinity, and now exists somewhere in the multidimensional vastness that is existence. But rather than just disappear, Earl faked his death so as to create a resolution here on earth and to leave his affairs in order. I feel sure he had this planned for a long time.

Now Earl is a Voodoo spirit who soars into the dreams of sorcerers and brings them knowledge of the strangeness that lies beyond our senses.

➤ TRANSCENDENCE ➤

New World spirituality – Voodoo, Santeria and Macumba – offers a powerful road to spiritual transcendence. The best way to access this is to call the Voodoo spirit Papa Legba, known in Santeria and Macumba as 'Eshu'.

To do this, place nine or more candles on your altar and light them. Then set up a crystal ball on your altar and perform a cleansing ritual. As usual, enter a mild trance, then stare into the crystal ball, uttering the invocation of Papa Legba *(below)*. Don't worry too much about what words you say. Just try and be familiar and friendly, so that in the end it becomes quite natural to talk out loud, despite the fact that you are seemingly alone in your room.

At some stage, you may well see something unusual appear in your crystal ball. If this occurs, follow it with your imagination. Using this method, you will eventually encounter Papa Legba, lord of the crossroads and opener of the gates. If you approach him with respect, and pass various tests he will likely set you, then you will be granted entrance into the spirit world. It is then a matter of destiny whether, in the long run, you achieve spiritual transcendence. There are no guarantees – but, take heart, the path is a noble one.

'Papa Legba, open the gate.
Legba who sits on the gate,
give us the right to pass into
the spirit world.'

TRICKSTER (SLIGHT RETURN)

Now my tale is coming to a close, I'd like to conclude with a story Earl told me. He heard it long ago in Mississippi and it involves the irrepressible Rabbit.

Rabbit was the smartest animal in the woods; but he wasn't satisfied. So he went to the king and asked for more sense. The king said he must bring him peas from a man's garden. Rabbit carefully cut a board off the man's garden fence, collected a bag of peas, and took them to the king. The king said that Rabbit was pretty smart, but that he should now bring him a buzzard's tail feather. Rabbit had a fox play dead, and when the buzzard, who was the undertaker in those parts, tried to carry it home, Rabbit snuck up and pulled out a handful of tail feathers. He took them to the king, who then told him he must bring a rattlesnake's poison fangs. Rabbit took a ball of sweetgum and covered it with partridge feathers. He tied it to a string and dragged it past a rattlesnake's home. Thinking it was a little partridge, that rattlesnake bit it, and its teeth stuck in the gum and wouldn't come loose. Rabbit said that the only way to get the rattlesnake loose was to break the teeth. Desperate to get free, the rattlesnake agreed. So Rabbit broke the teeth and took the ball of sweetgum, along with the teeth, to the king.

'There's no use in you asking for more sense,' said the king. 'I just am not going to give you more – because you have too much already!'

Like Rabbit, all Hoodoo doctors have a thirst for knowledge and wisdom; but maybe the mark of a true sorcerer is the ability to simply rest and wait, and listen to the whispers of the spirit, as it weaves its way around the edge of forever. In other words, every one of us has all the knowledge and wisdom we need inside, from the very day we are born. We just have to be still and listen to access it.

May luck and happiness be yours.
Doktor Snake, The Upside-Down Man
(*Visit me at* www.doktorsnake.com)

FURTHER READING

The Bluesman, Julio Finn. Northampton, MA: Interlink Publishing Group, 1998. If you want the real low-down on the blues, read this book. Finn, a black bluesman himself, shows how Voodoo and Hoodoo were central to the development of blues. He also provides an in-depth analysis of the Robert Johnson legend.

Hoodoo – Conjuration – Witchcraft – Rootwork, Harry M. Hyatt. Self published, 1978. Although currently out of print, copies can be picked up. It is a huge five-volume collection of folkloric material gathered by Hyatt in the southern states of America between 1936 and 1940. It contains over 13,000 separate magic spells and folkloric beliefs, plus lengthy interviews with professional root doctors, conjurors and hoodoos.

Legends of Incense, Herb and Oil Magic, Lewis de Claremont. Texas: Dorene Publishing, 1966. A strong influence on twentieth-century Hoodoo practices, this collection presents information about the basics of magical spell work involving roots, herbs, talismans, sachets, oils and incense.

Mules and Men, Zora Neale Hurston. New York, London: HarperPerennial, 1990. Hurston (1891–1960) was a novelist, folklorist and anthropologist, whose fictional and factual accounts of black heritage are unparalleled. This is a collection of wonderful folk tales, drawn from the southern states of America. It also has an extensive and fascinating section on Hoodoo – Hurston was actually instructed in the art of conjure by a number of Hoodoo doctors.

Papa Jim's Spellbook, James E. Sickafus. San Antonio, Texas: Papa Jim, 1997. Top class information on the practice of magic in the Voodoo, Hoodoo and Santeria traditions. Papa Jim also runs a spiritual supply store *(see opposite)*.

Voodoo and Hoodoo, Jim Haskins. New York: Original Publications, 1990. A collection of southern states conjure lore observed by the author during the 1960s and 70s. Haskins is a top black American journalist and writer, and this book is a must for anyone interested in the roots and contemporary practice of Hoodoo.

SUPPLIERS

All herbs, oils, roots, powders, mojo hands and Voodoo dolls mentioned in this book can be obtained from spiritual supply stores, known as botanicas. Books, audio tapes and CDs relating to Voodoo, Hoodoo and Santeria can also be obtained from these places. Here is a small selection of reputable stores. All are open for business Mondays to Saturdays and also provide mail order and on-line ordering services.

MANDRAGORA
(A division of Mandrake Press)
Essex House, Thame, OX9 3LS, UK.
Tel: 01844 260990
Fax: 01844 260991
E-mail: info@mandrake-press.com
Order online at:
www.mandrake-press.com

SCULLY ELLY'S VOODOO JOINT
Botanica and Spiritual Supplies
P.O. Box 770380, New Orleans,
Louisiana 70177-0380, USA.
Order online at:
www.thejukejoint.com/sculelvoodjo.html

PAPA JIM'S BOTANICA
5630 Flores Street, San Antonio,
TX 78214, USA.
Tel: 210-922-6665
E-mail: info@papajimsbotanica.com
Order online at:
http://papajimsbotanica.com/

BOTANICA ELEGUA
6043 Bissonnet, Houston,
TX 77081, USA.
Tel: 713-660-6767
E-mail: mrios@houston.rr.com
Order online at:
www.botelegua.com

NEW ORLEANS MISTIC
2267 St. Claude Avenue, New Orleans,
LA 70117, USA.
Tel: 504-944-5772
E-mail: info@neworleansmistic.com
Order online at:
www.neworleansmistic.com

INDEX

ACKNOWLEDGEMENTS

I would like to take this opportunity to thank all those who, under the auspicies of power itself, helped to bring this book into material manifestation. Thanks firstly must go to my beloved wife Nicky, who thoroughly read and criticized the typescripts and offered valuable suggestions. Thanks must also go to my two daughters, Audra and Imogen, whose abstract creative assistance both on and off the tabletop was of a remarkable nature. Gratitude must also be given to Felix Lejac, whose conjurations set the whole ball rolling. Great thanks must also go to Dr Dream, a formless creative whose help as a breathless being brought forth a critical change in the unseen energetic current of the spellbook.

Finally, let the Lord of the Strange and Savage Momentums offer his thanks to all the team at Eddison Sadd. Thanks in particular to Ian Jackson, Nick Eddison, Elaine Partington, Sophie Bevan and to Braz. Last, but not least, thanks to Chris Daunt for his vibrant and powerful artwork.

EDDISON•SADD EDITIONS

Editorial Director Ian Jackson
Editor Sophie Bevan
Indexer Dorothy Frame
Art Director Elaine Partington
Designer Brazzle Atkins
Illustrator Chris Daunt
Production Karyn Claridge and Charles James